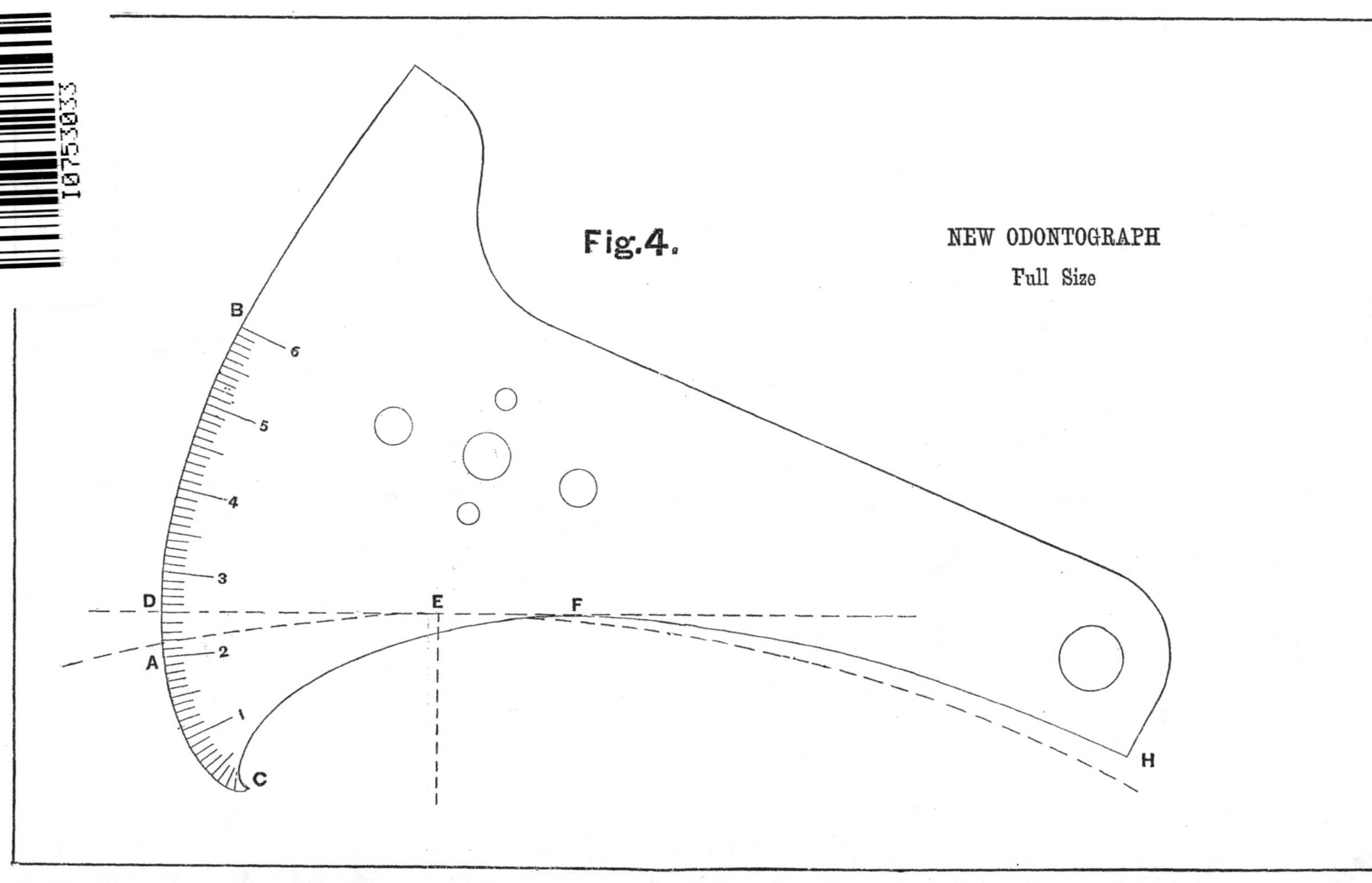

Fig. 4.

NEW ODONTOGRAPH
Full Size

I0753033

A

PRACTICAL TREATISE

ON THE

TEETH OF WHEELS

With the Theory and the use of

ROBINSON'S ODONTOGRAPH.

BY

S. W. ROBINSON,

Professor of Mechanical Engineering,

ILLINOIS INDUSTRIAL UNIVERSITY.

ILLUSTRATED.

NEW YORK:

D. VAN NOSTRAND, PUBLISHER,

23 MURRAY AND 27 WARREN STREET.

1876.

PREFACE.

The present little volume, reprinted from the pages of VAN NOSTRAND'S MAGAZINE, has resulted from an effort to bring before the mechanical public improved facilities for obtaining correct gearing.

Correct gear teeth are essential for the economic transmission of power, as well as extremely desirable for avoiding needless rattling. Many of the cast gears introduced into mills and factories may properly be termed rattling machines, and simply because the designer had too vague a conception of the theory of gearing, or because he sought to avoid the trouble of laying them out.

If this manual, and the odontograph, shall contribute toward relieving these inconveniences, the object sought, when the instrument was devised, and an effort made to present it in convenient form for use, will be realized.

S. W. R.

ILLINOIS INDUSTRIAL UNIVERSITY,
July, 1876.

PART I.

ON THE

THEORY OF GEAR TEETH.

AND ADAPTATION OF PARTICULAR FORMS FOR CERTAIN PURPOSES.

THOUGH the curves which may be employed for the outlines of mathematically correct gear teeth are infinite in number, varying greatly in external appearance, yet all of them must conform with one general principle, viz.: *tooth curves must transmit, from one shaft to the other, the same motion as would the pitch lines when acting by simple rolling contact.*

This truth is, in reality, axiomatic; and for the present purpose needs no discussion or comment. It forms the basis of the present investigation, the object of which is to show how the curves may differ, and the adaptation of certain ones for special purposes.

In this article the terminology indicated below is adopted.

The *pitch lines* of a pair of wheels are lines which pass near the mid-height of all the teeth, and separate the faces from the flanks. These lines must always exist, whether the wheels are designed with regard to them or not, and on which the tooth spaces of one wheel equal those of the other.

The *face* of a tooth is that part of the outline of one side of a tooth which extends from the point or top of tooth to the pitch line.

The *flank* of a tooth is that part of the outline of one side of a tooth which extends from the pitch line to the bottom of the space between two adjacent teeth. The length of this, reckoned in the direction of a radius, is usually made a little greater than the length of the face, similarly measured, to allow foi *clearance*.

The *pitch* is the distance, reckoned

on the pitch line, from a point on one tooth to the corresponding point on the next.

The *velocity-ratio* is the ratio of the angular velocities of the wheels, and may be constant or variable. If constant, it is equal to the number of revolutions per minute of one wheel, divided by the same for the other.

In the study of gearing two kinds of contact are considered, viz. : rolling contact and sliding contact. The former takes place between the pitch lines, and the latter between the curves forming the outlines of the teeth. When the pitch lines are not circular, the problem of determining them so as to give true rolling contact, with fixed axes, is quite extensive. The present paper is confined to the outlines of teeth, the pitch lines being supposed given.

In the figure, let A and B represent the centers of a pair of gears, and M N and O P the curves of a pair of teeth in action. The point of contact C is chosen at one side of the line of centers, so as to represent the general case.

Now, suppose the wheel A to swing through the small angle C A E. The

FIG. 1.

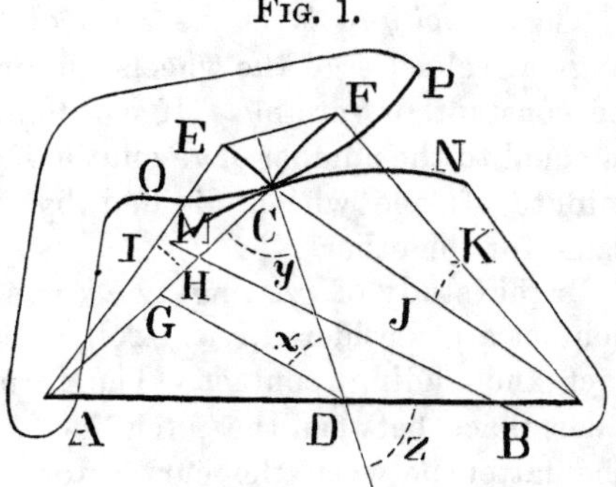

point C will describe the elementary arc C E. At the same time the wheel B, to maintain contact with A, must move through the elementary angle C B F, and C through the arc C F.

To determine C F, it is sufficient to note that as the movements of the wheels are elementary, the common tangent to the curves at C will scarcely change its inclination appreciably. Therefore, the end of the radius B C will be found at F, in a line, E F, parallel to the common tangent.

Draw a common normal C D to the curves. It will be perpendicular to E F. Then the velocity-ratio may be obtained as follows :

At a unit's distance from A and B draw H I and J K respectively. These arcs will serve to measure the angular velocities of the wheels, and hence :

$$\text{Velocity-ratio}=\frac{HI}{JK}.$$

The triangle C E F is similar to C D G, and hence :

$$
\begin{aligned}
AH &: AC :: HI : CE \\
BJ &: BC :: JK : CF \\
CE &: CF :: CG : DG \\
DG &: BC :: AD : AB \\
CG &: AC :: BD : AB
\end{aligned}
$$

Whence, observing that AH=BJ = unity,

$$\text{Velocity-ratio}=\frac{HI}{JK}=\frac{EC}{AC}\cdot\frac{BC}{CF}=\frac{CG}{DG}.$$

$$\frac{BC}{AC}=\frac{AB}{AD}\cdot\frac{BD}{AB}=\frac{BD}{AD}=\frac{V}{v}\text{*},$$

---

* This geometrical solution is essentially the

if V and v represent the angular velocities of A and B.

Hence, when rotary motion is transmitted from one shaft to another by sliding contact as in gear teeth, the angular velocities are to each other inversely as the segments, or parts of the line of centers, formed by its being cut by the common normal to the curves.

It is to be observed that at the end of

---

same as that given in Belanger's most excellent work on Cinematique, page 90, where also the velocity of sliding is found to be proportional to C D.

Those familiar with Trigonometry may prefer the following trigonometrical solution. We have

$$CE = AC \cdot V, \quad CF = BC \cdot v,$$

$$CEF = \text{angle } y, \quad CFE = x, \quad ADC = z;$$

and hence :

$$CE \sin. y = CF \sin. x,$$
$$AC \sin. y = AD \sin. z,$$
$$BC \sin. x = BD \sin. z,$$

or

$$V . AD \sin z = v . BD \sin. z,$$

and

$$\frac{V}{v} = \frac{BD}{AD},$$

as before.

the movements C E and C F, the points which were in mutual contact at C are now removed a distance E F; and as this displacement was accompanied with slipping, the amount of the latter is E F. In the similar triangles C E F and CDG, we have the same relation between E F and C D, as we have between C E and C G, or C F and G D. Hence, E F can only be zero when C D vanishes; or when the point of contact is on the line of centers. For this, the contact has changed from sliding to rolling; and, therefore, for rolling contact, the angular velocities are inversely as the radii of contact. In circular wheels the velocity-ratio must remain constant, because these segments are constant; whereas, in non-circular wheels it is variable. In the former, the point of contact remains fixed, while, for the latter, its position varies along the line A B.

The contact of a pair of teeth must continue for a time, at least, long enongh for the next pair of teeth to come fairly to contact; or, long enough for the pair of teeth to move through a space as great as the length of the pitch. This contact cannot therefore be confined to the line of centers, and hence sliding of the curves upon each other is unavoidable*.

From the preceding discussions it follows that in all gear wheels, circular or non-circular, the common normal to the sliding curves, and the pitch lines, must both maintain a common point of intersection with the line of centers ; and this condition is the only one necessary for fulfilling the general principle stated at the outset. The common normal, because it is the line of action of the pressure between the teeth, friction neglected, and, for its importance otherwise, is called the *line of action.*

Suppose, for example, any curve whatever, as $b\,a\,c$ Fig. 2, be taken as the

---

* Hooke's spiral gearing admits of contact which may be confined to the plane of the axes, and hence free from slip. But this is due, not to the form of tooth, but width of wheel face; or, length of wheel in direction of axis.

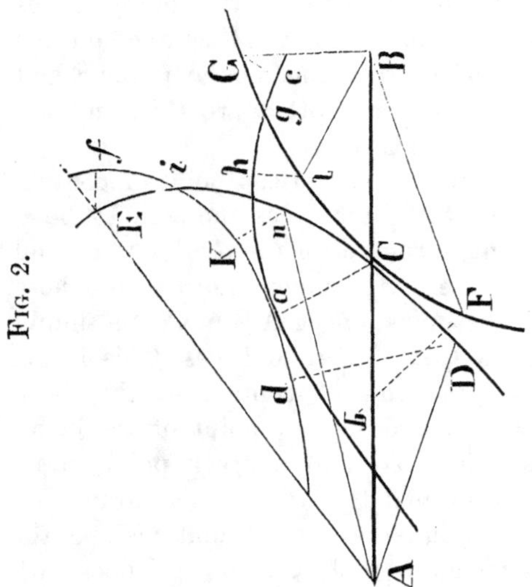

Fig. 2.

form of the side of a tooth of a gear wheel revolving about B. Then let the curve *d a f* be found for the side of a tooth of A, which, acting by sliding contact on *b a c*, will give to A the same angular motion as that transmitted by the rolling curves D E and F G, the latter being supposed circular or not. Let D and F be two points of the rolling curves which come to mutual contact on the line of centers, and similarly for E and G. Then arc C D = arc C F, and arc C E = arc C G, &c.

Now for the present point of contact C of the pitch lines there must be a point of contact of the tooth curves, and because the common normal to those curves must meet A B in C, we simply draw C *a*, normal to *b a c*. This is the present point of contact of the tooth curves, and hence a point of the curve sought. To find another point, draw F *b* normal to *b a c*. Then draw D *d* equal in length to F *b*, and making the same angle with A D, that F *b* does with B F prolonged. Then, *d* is a second point of the required curve ; because when D and F are in contact on the line A B, D *d* and F *b* will coincide in length and direction, with *d* and *b* superposed, forming the point of contact of the tooth-curves. In like manner *f*, and indeed any number of points may be found. The curve $d\,a\,f$, traced through these points, is the desired curve.*

In the above example, A and B are supposed to be the centers of rotation, in which case D E, and F G, must be a pair of correct rolling curves. But the solution is still more general. Any two curves whatever, without fixed axes even, may be used for the rolling curves. and the sliding curves determined. When radii do not exist, tangents to the rolling curves may be used to reckon the angles by. Such a case, however, would but rarely occur in practice.

This solution indicates that one tooth curve may be assumed, and the other formed as a dependence. It fails, however, as being both theoretically and mechanically impossible, and so with any theory, when the normals C *a*, F *b*, &c., will not strike the pitch line.

Though one tooth-curve may be assumed and the other determined, the

---

* This solution given in Belanger's Cinematique, p. 97, appears to be due to De la Hire; and given by him as early as 1694. See Willis' Princ. Mechanism, 2d ed., p. 89.

theory admits of other solutions; the most common being by aid of *describing* curves, called also *generating* or *tracing* curves. In this case the describing curve is assumed and both tooth-curves made dependent. To show that this solution depends upon one and the same general theory, let us find a describing curve which will generate the tooth-curve *b a c*, or *d a f*.

In Fig. 3 draw *g l* equal to *h l*, Fig. 2. Then take *l* C, Fig. 3, equal *l* C, Fig. 2. Also *g* C, Fig. 3, equal *a* C, Fig. 2. And again C F and *g* F, Fig. 3, equal C F and *b* F, Fig. 2, respectively, &c., for as many points as desired. Then trace the curve *g l* C F, Fig. 3. This is the describing curve sought. Now suppose this curve be placed in contact with F G, Fig. 2, so that *g*, Fig. 3, falls at *g*, Fig.

FIG. 3.

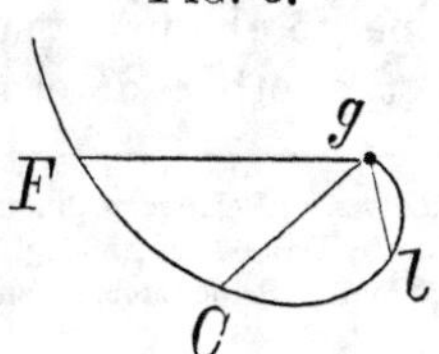

2. Then by rolling the describing curve along toward F, the points *l*, C, F, Fig. 3 will exactly fall at *l*, C, F, Fig. 2, because the arcs *g l*, *l* C, C F, are equal in the two figures. Also the construction makes *g l*, *g* C, *g* F, &c., intersect the arc of the describing curve at the same angles that the normals *h l*, *a* C, *b* F, &c., intersect the pitch line, which is easily seen to be true by supposing the points *g*, C, F, &c., very numerous. Hence the radii vectors of Fig. 3 will successively come to exact coincidence with the normals of Fig. 2, and at the same time *g* will trace out the very curve *g h a b*.* And similarly, by rolling the same curve from *i* to D, Fig. 2, the curve *i k a d* will be traced. In like manner a describing curve can be produced which will generate, by rolling from *g* or *i* toward G or E, the remaining portions *g e* and *i f* of the tooth-curves.

Thus it appears that a generating curve can always be found that will trace out a given tooth-curve. But

* De la Hire, in 1733.

whenever the latter are neither of them fixed, we are at liberty to assume a describing curve, and this may be of any form whatever which may admit of rolling on the pitch lines. The two solutions are therefore one and the same, the difference being simply in the part assumed. And within this are comprehended all known forms of gearing, such as involute, epicycloidal, epitrochoidal, pin-gearing, Prof. Edward Sang's hour glass curve gearing, &c., &c.

The solution of the problem is therefore reduced to simply this; any describing curve rolled upon the outside of one pitch line, and upon the inside of the other pitch line, beginning at mutual contact points; will describe a pair of faces and flanks which will work correctly.

This may be demonstrated by a direct graphical method as follows.

Take pitch lines A D and B E, circular or non-circular, and a describing curve C A H; or, which is the same, K B I. Also take D and E as the pair

FIG. 4.

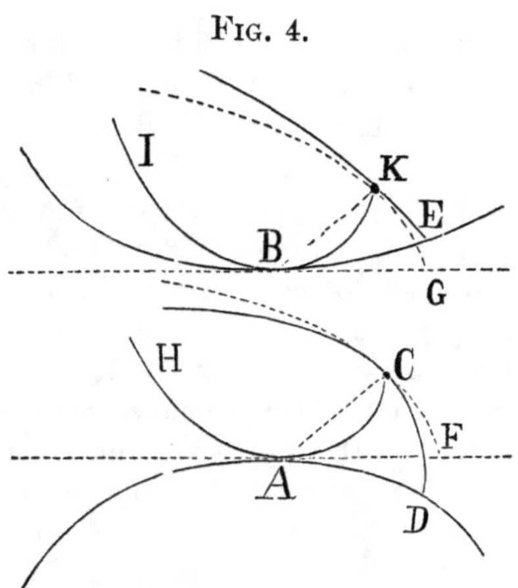

of mutual contact points, where the pair of tooth-curves sought begin. Let C A H roll in outside contact from D to A, describing D C by a tracing point C ; and similarly rolling the same curve from E to B, describes the curve E K. This rolling may be continued to any extent, giving the full line curves D C, and E K produced.

If the same curve be rolled on tangents at A and B, two equal curves will be described which are shown in dotted lines. Let arc D A = arc E B = arc C A = arc K B = A F = B G. Then chord A C = chord B K, and angle C A F = angle K B G. Hence if A and B be placed in tangential contact, the tangents and dotted curves will coincide precisely ; and the full line curves, or tooth-curves, will have a point of tangency at C K. Also the curves will not pass, one to the opposite side of the other, because the full line curve for A lies wholly below, and for B wholly above the mutually coinciding dotted curves. This being true for one point taken at random must be true for all, giving the precise conditions required for tooth-curves.

We might suppose for illustration that the three curves roll upon each other with one point A, Fig. 5, in common tangency. The tracing point C, would then trace, simultaneously, the two curves shown, one upon the plane of each wheel, which will serve to work correctly as a face and flank.

Fig. 5.

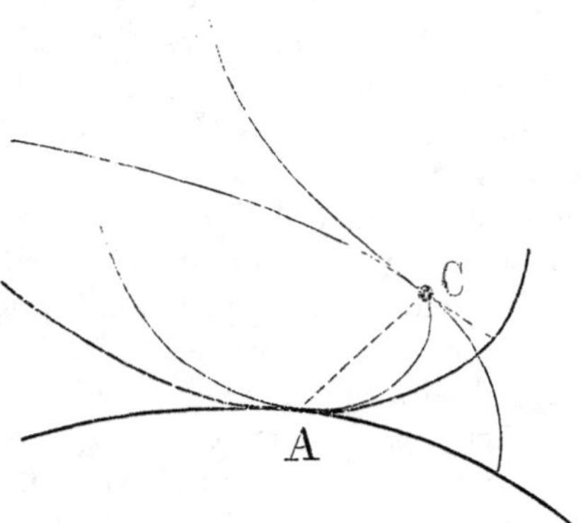

We are now prepared to draw the following conclusions :

1st. The faces and flanks all have their origins at the pitch line.

2d. Each face and flank couplet must be generated by rolling the tracing curve in the same direction, on the outside of one, and inside of the other pitch line.

3d. The contact of a couplet is confined to one side of the line of centers.

4th. Couplets which do not interchange flanks and faces may be generated by different describing curves; even though on the same pair of wheels.

Different describing curves give different forms of gear teeth, some of the most important of which will now be considered.*

In practice the pitch lines are usually circular; though on shaping and slotting machines, and others requiring a "quick return," non-circular wheels have been employed with advantage. In Fig. 6 is given such a pair of non-circular wheels, drawn carefully to a scale, with each tooth-curve worked out for its particular position by the general theory.† The describing curve used was a circle, the diameter of which was about one-third that of the pitch line of A. These wheels were designed with special reference to

* It may be observed by comparing Figs. 2, 3 and 5 that the generating eurve must lie on the opposite side of the pitch line from where the inte sections of the normals are found. From this it follows that if these intersections cross the pitch line as the rolling proceeds, so must the describing curve. The latter will then change its direction with a cusp.

† Drawn by a former pupil, Mr. Emory Patch.

Fig. 6.

adaptation for shaping and slotting machines, in which the tool is reciprocated by a crank and pitman. The forward stroke is uniform, except for one-fourteenth at each end, given for slowing down for passing the center. The return is accomplished in one-half the time the entire forward stroke requires. The teeth are made large, proportionately, for the purpose of illustrating the fact that such wheels require teeth which differ from each other in form.

Circular wheels form only a special case of the general theory ; but as these are of almost exclusive use in practice, with the teeth varied for different purposes, the following important classes will be considered separately, viz.:

I. Wheels with epicycloidal teeth ;
II. Wheels with involute teeth ;
III. Wheels with random teeth.

Epitrochoidal curves have been suggested for tooth-curves, but as they do not admit of tooth-contacts near the line of centers, where most desirable, they are not useful for general purposes.

I. EPICYCLOIDAL GEARING.

This name is applied because the tooth-curves are epicycloids and hypocycloids. An epicycloid is traced by a point upon the plane of a circle, when that point is guided by being attached to the circumference of a second circle which rolls upon the first. If external it is an epicycloid, if internal an hypocycloid.

A curious fact relating to these curves deserves notice, viz.: that every epicycloid and hypocycloid admits of being generated by two different rolling circles. To illustrate, suppose A *b c* to be a primitive or pitch circle, and B a rolling or describing circle, tracing with *p* the epicycloid D, by rolling on A. Draw the line *p b c* through the point of tangency *b*. Then *b p* will be a normal to the epicycloid at *p*, because an elementary part of the latter is described while *b* serves as an instantaneous axis for the wheel B to turn about. Now, this elementary portion of D will be the same if *c* be the center instead of *b*. This being true for each elementary part of D, it follows that a circle C, tangent at c, and having a tracing point p, will trace the same epicycloid that B will. It can be easily

FIG. 7.

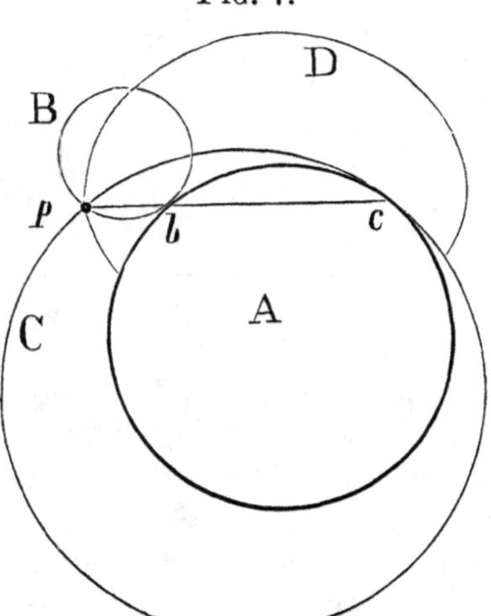

shown that the difference of the diameters of C and B is equal to the diameter of A.*

* Due to Duhamel, see Bour Cours de Cinematique, p. 120.

Fig. 8 indicates how this double generation applies to the hypocycloid, in which A is the pitch circle and B the

FIG. 8.

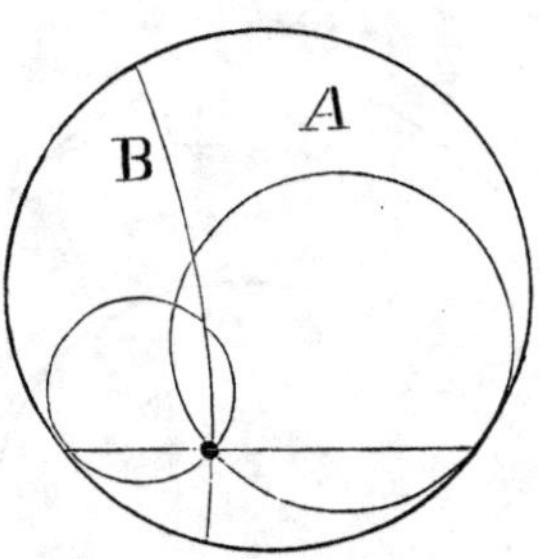

hypocycloid. The sum of the two diameters of the generating circles evidently equal the diameter of the pitch circle.

That the teeth be mechanically possible, it is necessary that the generating circles be as small, or smaller than the pitch circles within which they roll; otherwise the teeth would be much undercut.

This range in the relation of sizes gives variety of form of teeth, the following of which are the most essential :

1st. Flanks radial.
2d. Flanks parallel, for strength.
3d. For minimum of friction.
4th. For change-gears and sets.
5th. Pin gearing.

1ST. EPICYCLOIDAL TEETH WITH RADIAL FLANKS.

Suppose a generating circle to roll inside a pitch circle, with the diameter of the former equal to the radius of the latter. By reference to Fig. 8 we see that the two generating circles would be equal, and the hypocycloid a straight line, a diameter of the pitch circle. This principle is the foundation of the well-known White's parallel motion.

Hence when the diameters of the generating circles equal the radii of the pitch circles in which they roll, the flanks will be radial, and very convenient to construct. In practice, therefore, we have simply to delineate the epicycloids, with circles half as large as the opposite pitch circles, and strike in the tangent radii for flanks. This form of gearing is the most convenient for practical execution of any good form known, and for this reason is the form usually adopted, when correct delineation is attempted. Indeed many designers have no idea of the existence of any other correct form, except, possibly, the involute.

Fig. 9 represents the simultaneous generation of the faces and flanks for both wheels, the four circles being supposed

Fig. 9.

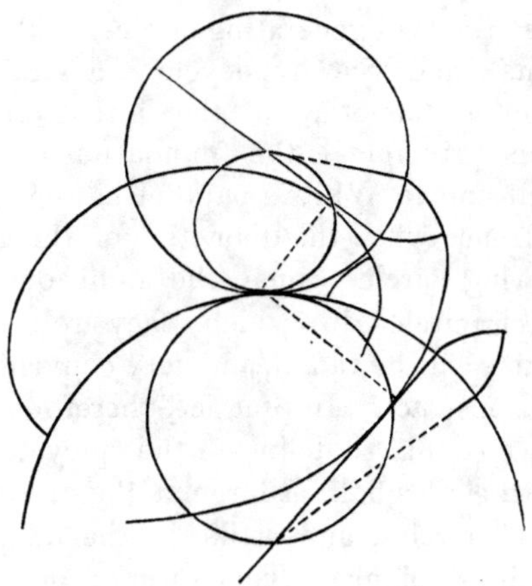

to roll upon each other with only one point in common, each tracing point describing two lines.

In wheels of few teeth, the latter appear somewhat undercut, and weakened, when the flanks are drawn wholly radial.

But it is easily demonstrated that a face works upon only a small portion of the flank, which also is adjacent to the pitch line. Below this the teeth may be thickened by clearance curves, almost entirely removing this objection. An advantage is gained by these teeth which probably more than compensates for the above objection. This consists in the great freedom from crowding of the wheels from each other, due to the near approach of the line of action to the perpendicular to the line of centers ; and this is evidently necessary for most favorably transmitting the rotative forces from one wheel to the other. For instance if the line of action be made parallel to the line of centers no rotative effect is secured.

2D. FLANKS PARALLEL.

By employing smaller generating circles than in the above the flanks may be rendered more nearly parallel as shown in Fig. 10 ; and the bases of the teeth

FIG. 10.

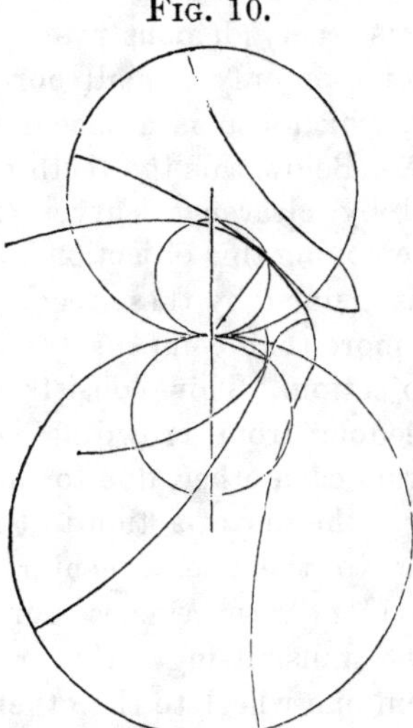

thickened as required for strength. Clearing curves may still be introduced for further strengthening of the teeth.

No rule of proportions is prescribed : in each case the diameters of the rolling circles must be determined by the judgment of the designer.

The flanks are only approximately parallel, because, in reality, they are the slightly curved hypocycloids. But for that small part against which the faces act, a straight line may be substituted without sensible error.

The rolling circles being smaller than for the case of radial flanks, the epicycloids will be smaller for the same pitch lines, and hence the points of the teeth narrower. This results in a greater general inclination of the side of a tooth to a radius, causing greater inclination of the line of action from the perpendicular to the line of centers, inducing increased lateral crowding, and consequent friction. In a long train of gearing it is therefore doubtful whether this form of tooth is any safer than the preceding, because with greater strength there is greater resistance.

3D. FOR MINIMUM OF FRICTION.

From the preceding examples, it appears that the friction is reduced by approaching the line of action to the perpendicular to the line of centers. The line of action in epicycloidal teeth being the chord to the generating circle which connects the describing point with the point of rolling, it appears that the most favorable condition is secured by making the generating circles large as possible.

Again the generating circles, when situated as in Figs. 9, 10 and 11, form the path of the points of contact in their journey from the point of beginning, to the point of quitting contact, one circle for one side and the other for the opposite side of the line of centers; so that large circles, in both senses, appear most favorable.

Fig. 11 presents these conditions, and indicates that the teeth are very much undercut; indeed, in extreme cases, entirely cut off by reason of the convex flanks, due to the excessively large rolling circles.

Fig. 11.

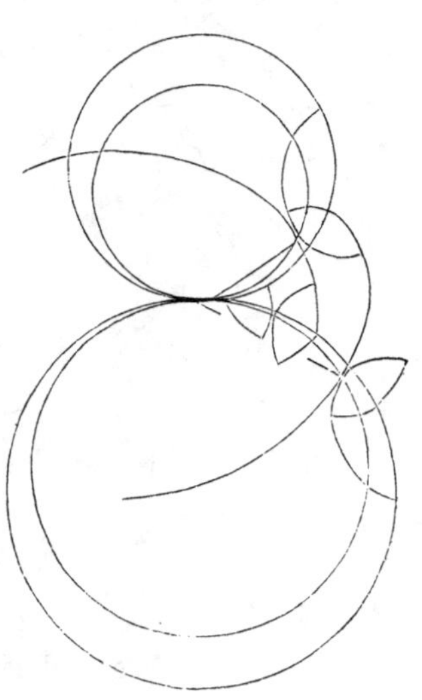

It is evident that such teeth cannot be used where great strength is required, as in mill-work ; but where the resistance is slight, and smoothness of motion and freedom of action are requisites, as in horology, this form may be used with great advantage. Fig. 12 is a careful

Fig. 12.

drawing of such a pair of wheels, with teeth much undercut.

4TH. CHANGE GEARS, AND SETS.

The most common use of change gears occurs with the machinist's engine lathe for screw-cutting. In this, and most other cases requiring such wheels, the teeth are small ; and when only approximate, occasion no especial inconvenience. But sets sometimes occur in mill-gearing where correct forms of teeth are necessary.

For such cases it is only needful that *one* generating circle be employed for the whole set.* This circle should not be more than half as large as the smallest wheel of the set. The teeth of the latter will then have radial flanks, while those of all the others have concave flanks and thick bases.

5TH. PIN GEARING.

By increasing the generating circle, Fig. 11, the hypocycloid decreases until, when the former coincides with the pitch circle, the latter becomes a point, the tracing point itself. Then the theoretical teeth are points for one wheel, and for the other epicycloids generated by the opposite pitch circle as shown in Fig. 13. In practice the points are en-

* This solution was first given by Prof. Willis, see Princ. of Mech., 2d ed., pp. 87, 118, and 136, the latter as in connection with the Willis Odontograph.

Fig. 13.

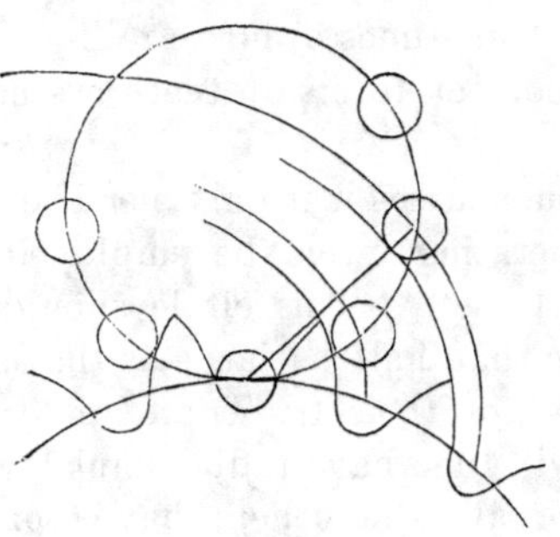

larged to pins of cylindrical form, and the teeth reduced to lines parallel to the epicycloids and distant from them a space equal to the radius of the pin. Such wheels are sometimes called pin gearing.

These wheels should work smoothly, because the line of action is suitably situated for a minimum of friction, but they are not free from objection for having the tooth contacts all on one side of the line of centers. These one-sided contacts serve best when the pin wheel is driven, and in this way this gearing is much used in modern clock-work. The pinion, called *wallower*, *trundle* or *lantern wheel*, is usually made for clocks by inserting wires between two collars; while the wheels are cut from plates, many of which are stacked and cut at once.* In this way should the wheel be quite thin, and wabble, the trundle may have sufficient length of pins to accommodate. Such gearing is cheaper than thick cut gearings, and may explain its introduction into the inexpensive, though very good, American clocks.

But it is probable that the very best conditions for clock and watch gearing would be secured by a sort of *cross* between Figs. 11 and 13, represented in Fig. 14. The generating circle should be so large that the hypocycloid, for both pitch lines, spans a breadth just sufficient for the tooth thickness, and the whole hypocycloid taken as that part of a tooth, or pin, which lies within the pitch line. The balance of the tooth

* In the full sense of the term *pin gearing* the wheel teeth are also pins set into the edge of a disk.

should then extend outward, to a point, similarly as in Fig. 11. Thus contacts

FIG. 14.

will be secured on both sides of the line of centers, as required, with the nearest approach of the line of action to the perpendicular to the line of centers consistent therewith.

These wheels could be constructed by inserting suitably formed pins by one end into disks, and projecting toward each other from the two wheels ; or, by supporting the teeth upon slender necks, as shown, which is possible, because only small parts of the hypocycloids are brought into contact with the faces.

It is plain that if the line of action could be straight, and perpendicular to the line of centers, the wheels could be approached or withdrawn without causing great changes of conditions of action of the teeth. The form, Fig. 14, with teeth supported upon clearance curve-necks, would, therefore, be one of the best for this purpose, and nearly the same as found on the rollers of clothes-wringing machines, &c., as arrived at, probably, by the demands of practice.

II. INVOLUTE TEETH.

The involute curve is a special case of the epicycloid in which the generating circle is infinite.

Let A and B represent two pitch circles in contact at C. Draw any inclined right line through C and two circles tangent to it with centers A and B. These are taken as the base circles for

Fig. 15.

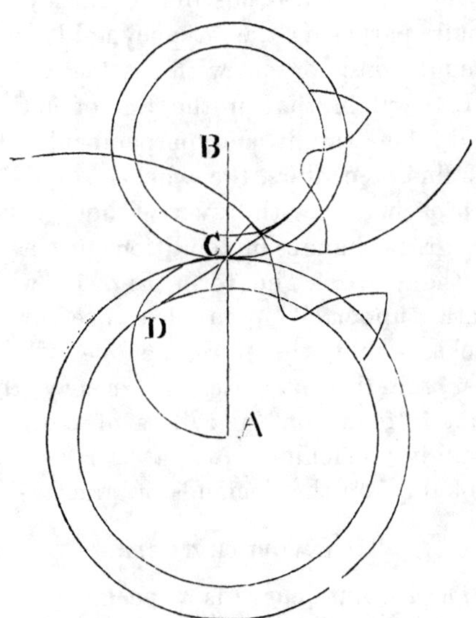

involutes. The ratio of the radii of these circles will be equal to that of the pitch circles. Suppose the inclined line, C D, be produced, and wound upon the base circle A; and also separated near C, with a tracing point attached. As the string is unwound, the tracing point will describe an involute which may be taken for the side of a tooth of A as shown. A similar unwinding from B will describe the involute tooth-curve for it. It is plain that the contacts will all lie on the inclined line C D, because it will cut normally all the involutes described on the bases A and B. This is at once the line of action, and locus of the points of contact.

In the present case the line of action is inclined more or less, at pleasure, but must always pass C. This change of inclination may follow from varying the diameters of either the pitch or base circles. The former corresponds to changing the distance between the axes of the wheels, which these gears are well known to admit of, and work correctly. But when the distance is considerable, the teeth become monstrous thick at base, and objectionable ; and unsuited for such purposes as clothes-wringers. The contact for these teeth is only possible between the points of tangency of the line of action with the base-circles. Hence, by enlarging the base-circles, these limits are constricted, and, finally, vanishing when the line of action becomes perpendicular to the line of centers, giving no contact. The best condition is a matter of judgment, and the designer must choose between objectionably few contacts, and objectionable inclination of line of action and thick teeth.

The contact being confined to the line of action, limited as above, it is plain that no bearing can occur upon a tooth below or inside the base circle, and usually clearance curves are arbitrarily struck in to give the necessary depth for receiving the points of the teeth of the other wheel.

One fact is worthy of note, serving to put these wheels in comparison with the epicycloidal. If a circle be struck with A C as diameter, it will always pass the point of tangency D. That point, in involute gearing, is the limit of contact of teeth ; but not in epicycloidal gearing with radial flanks, though that will be one position. Intermediate between D and C the contact for involutes is on the line C D; and for epicycloids, on the arc C D. The line of action in the latter case will vary from a perpendicular to A B, to the inclination C D, while the point of contact moves from C to D. Hence, the average inclination of the line of action between C and D is much more favorable in epicycloidal gearing than involute, from which it appears that the former is the preferable form of gearing.

Fig. 15 may appear to furnish an example which is inconsistent with our general theory, because the generation is effected by rolling the describing curve or line on the base circle instead of the pitch line. But this is reconciled thus: In Fig. 16 take a pitch circle A C, base circle B D, describing line D F, with describing point F, and a log. spiral F A. Now as the describing line unwinds, tracing the curve C F, the line will cut the pitch circle at various points A at a constant angle, which follows from the concentricity of the pitch and base circles. As the radius-vector makes a constant angle with the arc of a log. spiral if that angle at A, be the same as D F with the circle at A, then the radius vector F A will coincide with the line D F continually, and the tracing point will describe one and the same curve whether carried by the spiral F A or line F D. This curve begins at C. To supply the remaining part C B roll the same spiral

Fig. 16.

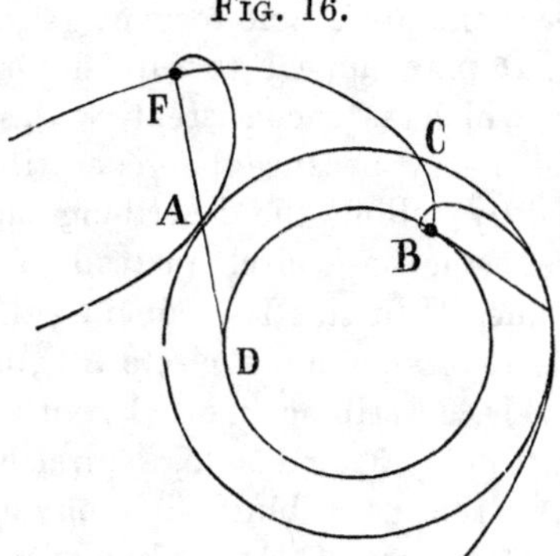

inside as shown. This description will stop at B for the reason that the log.

spiral then bears on the inside of the circle where its curvature equals that of the circle. Hence this is explained by the general theory, and the wheel has true flanks and faces, separated by the pitch line, as usual.

III. RANDOM TEETH.

These might be styled *random teeth* because a tooth-curve for one wheel is drawn at random, or at least arbitrary, and the form of tooth for the other wheel found from it. The solution on the drawing board is the same as Fig. 2, and hence, it is in keeping with the general theory of the teeth of wheels. It would need no further consideration except for the exceedingly advantageous practical process for obtaining the second curve, first made known by Prof. Willis in 1837.

Let A and B represent the pitch lines, formed by cutting strips to the right curves. A tooth curve C is cut at pleasure, and mounted on A so that the card board D may play between A and

FIG. 17.

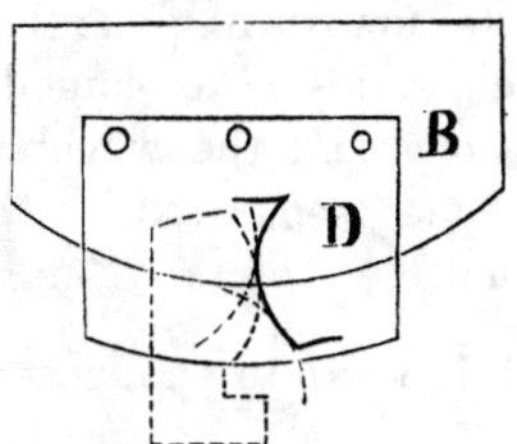

C. The card board D is secured to B. The pitch lines are then placed in contact as shown by the dotted lines, and a line traced on D, along the edge of C. Then

FIG. 18

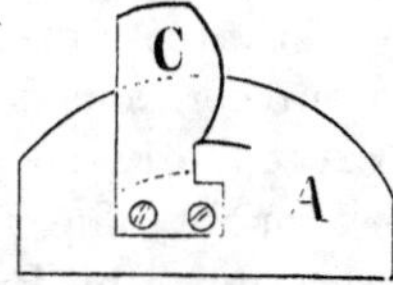

A is rolled on B, without slipping, to a new position, and a second line traced by the edge of C. Thus proceed for various positions. An enveloping curve traced on D will be the required tooth-curve for B.

This process would apply admirably for matching a gear already existing, and no matter if it be worn provided it is regular.

PRACTICAL OPERATIONS.

In actually executing wheel-work, there are certain operations which contribute to the accuracy and dispatch. The draughtsman can draw his tracing curve in several positions, and by stepping with spacing dividers arrive at several points in the desired tooth-curves. But in thus measuring off distances on arcs, errors occur in that the dividers measure chords instead of arcs. Also each placing of the divider points involves a small error depending upon eyesight, precision of draughtsman, &c., Again several operations, following and depending upon each other, between the theory and the result, entail cumulative errors, sometimes so great, that the result obtained scarcely resembles the truth. The fewer the intervening operations, the less will the truth be adulterated with error.

Templates are valuable because they secure a more direct relation between the theory and final tooth-curves. In some instances a still closer relation has been obtained. To illustrate, the templates give the curve, and then the teeth or cutters are to be formed from it by an eye-and-hand process. But in some watch-works, epicycloidal machines are used in which the cutters are formed direct from the rolling curves. These cutters however are *master cutters* from which the working cutters are formed. But this last operation admits of great precision.

In Fig. 17, the pieces A and B are called pitch templates and a piece cut to the form of the describing curve as in Fig. 3, is called a describing template.

By a set of such templates the operation represented in Fig. 4 may be undertaken. Tooth-curves may thus be drawn on metal plates, and subsequently cut carefully to the line. Such a pattern may be used for turning up a cutter by, or for marking out the teeth on a gear pattern of wood. In the latter case, it may be called a scribe template. And it is convenient to mount this upon a rod attached to swing around a center pin to the gear. Either of these operations involves two eye-and-hand processes, as, for instance, dressing up the scribe template; and then turning the cutter by it. But it is not convenient to reduce the number further, though, by aid of an *odontograph*, described in Part II of this number, the inconvenience of resorting to pitch and describing templates, is avoided from the fact that the odontograph serves as a ready-made scribe template, as exact as a special scribe template laid out and dressed up, as above described, would be, and which is also adapted to being mounted to swing around the center of the gear.

PART II.

ON A

NEW ODONTOGRAPH:

An Instrument for laying out

THE TEETH OF GEAR WHEELS.

THE WILLIS ODONTOGRAPH.

THOSE who have used, or even studied the *Odontograph* of Professor Willis, of Cambridge, England, cannot be otherwise than forcibly impressed with the admirable simplicity and great utility of the instrument. Indeed, it has attained to such general favor that it is not only in the hands of a large proportion of the constructors of mill gearing in Europe and America, but in every work of importance on Cinematics, Principles of Mechanism, Machinery and Millwork,

&c., published since its discovery in 1838. In fact, the instrument is worthy of a place in the tool chest of every millwright and machinist; particularly those who have no better understanding of the mode of delineating gear teeth, than to use, for generating the faces of teeth with radial flanks, describing circles which are the opposite pitch circles themselves, instead of circles one-half as large.

Although the teeth of wheels, laid out by the aid of the odontograph, are only approximately correct, such teeth are not very far from correct working forms. This fact was practically demonstrated to the writer at the justly-celebrated machine factory of Wm. Sellers & Co., of Philadelphia, where a pair of heavy cut gears were seen in action, running with extraordinary quietness. On inquiry as to the remarkable working quality of these gears, it was stated that the cutters were made expressly for them in strict conformity with the Willis odontograph; which, in the present instance, it is fair to suppose, was an experiment to test the odontograph teeth, as compared with those laid down correctly by theory. Teeth formed thus carefully, even though they be only approximate, are much to be preferred to the rattling, guess shapes; and amply repay the trouble required to secure them. It is therefore much better, in cases where the theory of gearing is not understood, to resort to an odontograph, than to jump blindly at a rattle trap.

For example : a common form among millwrights is obtained by taking the middle point of a tooth at the pitch line for a center, and describing, by arcs of circles, the nearest flanks of the next adjacent teeth, and the further faces of the same two teeth. Describing, thus four arcs from the center of each tooth, all the faces and flanks are laid out. This gives flanks which are concave, with radii which are less than those of the convex faces, while the opposite relation is known to be required in correctly laid out teeth. This rule probably gives shapes which are worse than mere guess shapes.

A GOOD ODONTOGRAPH DESIRABLE.

The delineation of correct working gear teeth according to theory for individual cases is a very easy matter when the method is understood, but not so easy as to use a convenient odontograph ; and hence, a good odontograph is advantageous to all designers of gearing.

ESSENTIAL QUALITIES OF A GOOD ODONTOGRAPH.

An odontograph, to give the highest satisfaction, should be one which leaves nothing to be desired ; neither in the degree of approximation, nor the general form of tooth it gives.

Those who have employed the odontograph of Prof. Willis, cannot fail to have noticed that in wheels of many teeth the form is very different from that obtained by laying out the teeth of the epicycloidal form with radial flanks,* which form is the most common and usually the most acceptable. Also the odontograph must be simple, and easy of application.

PECULIARITIES OF THE WILLIS ODONTOGRAPH TOOTH.

A tooth of a wheel of eighty teeth, as laid down by aid of the Willis odontograph, is shown in Fig. 1; and also, a little to one side in dotted lines, the same tooth of epicycloidal form with radial flanks, as calculated to work with a second wheel of twelve teeth. The clearance curves are not put in. The odontograph tooth exhibits very marked peculiarities, a noticeable one being the greater general inclination of the side of the odontograph tooth to the radius of the wheel; giving rise to unnecessary

* When these teeth would appear too weak at the root or base, *clearance curves* are usually struck in, or curves between the flanks which the points of the teeth of the opposite wheel will just clear, up to which the roots of the teeth may be thickened for the purpose of greater strength.

obliquity of action, and consequent mutual crowding of the wheels against their shafts.

Fig. 1.

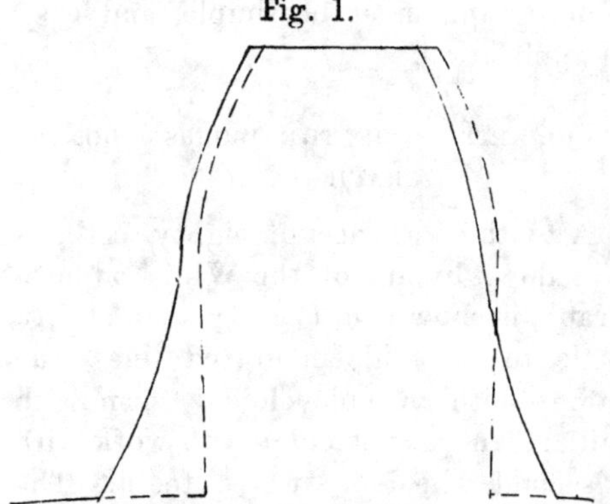

Prof. Willis limits his odontograph to twelve teeth for the least number, and for this the teeth have radial flanks as shown in Fig. 2, which works with a wheel of eighty teeth. This limitation causes the teeth of small wheels to be narrow at the base, and of large wheels to be unnecessarily wide. In wheels having a not unusually large number of teeth, the flanks start out from the pitch line towards the center with a divergence from each other approaching 30°.* In

Fig. 2.

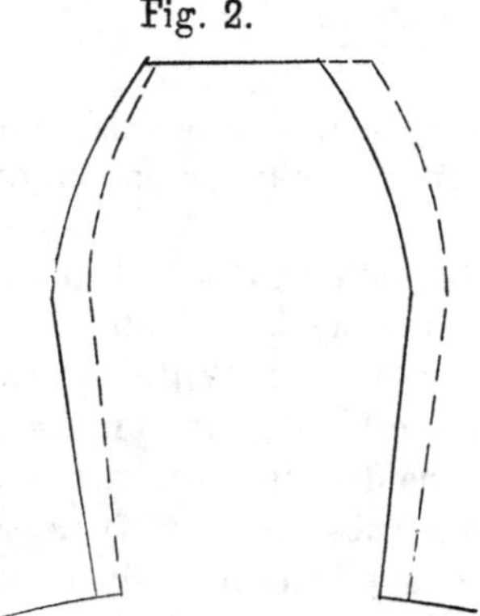

other words, the odontograph teeth approach the narrowness of base of epicycloidal teeth with radial flanks when the latter are objectionably narrow, as in wheels of few teeth ; and much wider, indeed excessively wide, when, for the same wheels, epicycloidal teeth are of good form. Also a marked peculiarity,

* See Fairbairn, Mills and Millwork, Part II, Plate IX, Fig. 1. A. Lambert, Cinematique, Pl. 14. M. CH. Viry Cours de Méchanique, p. 194, Fig. 30.

as exhibited in Fig. 2, is the decided angular junctions of the flanks and faces.

RESTRICTION OF THE WILLIS THEORY, AND MODIFIED FORM OF ODONTOGRAPH.

These undesirable features are, however, in the main, no fault of the general theory of Prof. Willis for the formation of teeth with circular arcs, but appear to be due to restrictions imposed, for the purpose of simplifying the tables for, and application of, the odontograph itself. The restrictions which contribute mostly to this are the fixed angle of 75°, and the constant length, relatively to the pitch, of the perpendicular to the line of action. By restricting the theory in a different manner, a certain modification of the instrument and its application may be effected, which gives straight and more nearly radial flanks for all wheels, and circle arc faces. This will be treated further on.

NEW FORM OF ODONTOGRAPH.

For those who will adopt nothing which is so incomplete as a circle arc for a tooth face, but will lay down the correct curves; and for even the less theoretical who would prefer to accept a good practical *short-cut* to a correct result than to go by guess; I would offer the new odontograph, which is now to be described: an instrument which in no circle arc, mode or form, resembles any thing above referred to.

This new form of odontograph is not only adapted to give radial flanks, but faces which agree with almost undiscoverable nearness with the epicycloidal face. The face curve, as laid down by the instrument, is exactly normal to a tangent to the pitch line drawn from the middle point of a tooth, and it intersects the addendum circle precisely where the true epicycloidal curve proper to the tooth in question does.

Now, as the pitch line and its tangent, pass either way from the middle of the tooth, they depart from each other slightly in distance, and more so in direction. A circle arc, approximating to a tooth face, will generally have a radius considerably greater than the half thickness of a tooth: but for a circle arc to be normal to the above-named tangent and to the pitch circle at the side of a tooth, both at the same time, its radius must be much less than the half thickness of a tooth, as is evident on inspection; and hence, the circle arc cannot osculate closely with the epicycloid, and at the same time be normal to the pitch circle, as Figs. 1 and 2 show. The most closely osculating curve must, therefore, be one which rapidly changes curvature; and such a curve will be very nearly normal to the above mentioned tangent to the pitch circle.

The odontograph should, therefore, give a curve which changes curvature rapidly. Now, as the epicycloidal curve is normal to the pitch line, and very nearly so to the tangent to the pitch circle drawn from the middle of a tooth, it is clear that if a curve of rapidly changing curvature be so placed as to be normal to the tangent, as above described, and at the same time intersecting the addendum circle at the same point that the epicycloidal curve required for the tooth considered does, it will represent the epicycloidal tooth face with great precision. This truth is rendered apparent to the eye in Fig. 3, in which the full line is the odontograph curve, and the dotted line the required epicycloid. The flank is also drawn in to give an idea of the conformity of the whole tooth, as delineated by aid of the instrument, with the true epicycloidal tooth. These teeth belong to a wheel, the pair of which are of equal size. The object of making the curve perpendicular or normal to the tangent, as above described, instead of the pitch circle, is to render the odontograph more convenient of application; and it is found that the curve selected, in the manner hereafter explained, meets the radius for extending the side of the tooth into the

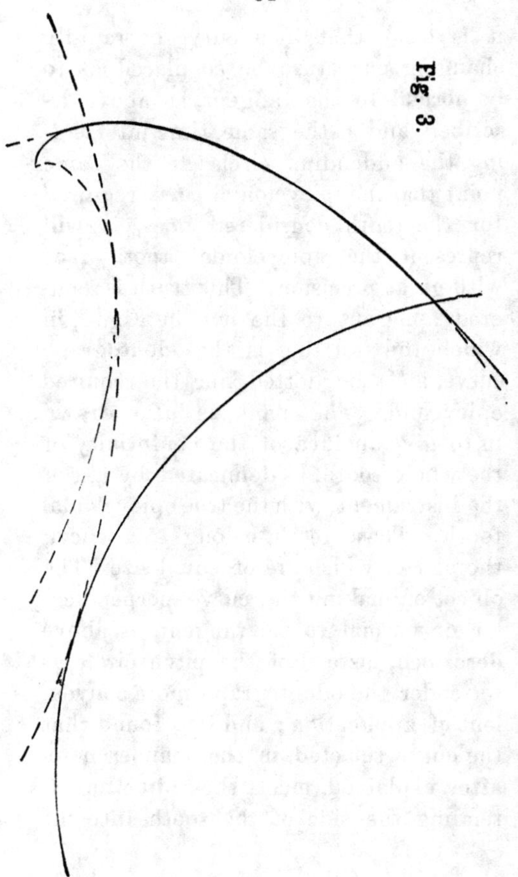

Fig. 3.

flank with an error of tangency, which is too small to be readily detected.

With these explanations, it becomes evident that the leading propositions of the new odontograph are:

1st. That it give a curve of rapidly changing curvature, having the closest possible osculation with the epicycloid, and at the same time be of general application.

2d. That the curve for a tooth face, given by the instrument, be normal to a tangent line to the pitch circle at the middle of a tooth.

3d. That this curve intersect the addendum circle precisely where the epicycloidal curve proper to the tooth in question does.

FORM OF CURVE ADOPTED.

The curve adopted as conforming most closely, in general, with limited initial portions of the epicycloid, is the *logarithmic spiral.*

This curve appears to possess the highest degree of adaptation, because of its uniform rate of change of curvature, and also because this rate can be assumed at pleasure.* Furthermore, the analytical relation of this spiral to the problem is simple.

FORM AND APPLICATION OF INSTRUMENT.

In planning this odontograph, the leading endeavor was to make its practical application the most convenient possible, without a sacrifice from accuracy of form of tooth obtained by it.

That the reader may learn the leading features of the instrument before proceeding to the details of its demonstration, its form and mode of application will first be explained.

The odontograph is shown full size in Fig. 4, as of suitable capacity for laying out all teeth below six inches pitch. Its capacity, however, is extended to any degree by simply prolonging the curved edges. It should be made of metal, be-

* These points follow from the fact that limited portions falling within a given angle at the pole are similar figures.

cause it is intended that the instrument, when desired, may be used directly for a scribe template, in which use it will be subject to wear from the passes of the scribe. It has several holes countersunk on both sides as shown, so that it may be attached by wood screws, or by bolts expressly prepared, to any convenient wooden rod, in such a manner that when the rod swings around a center-pin to the wheel, all the faces of the teeth may be described directly from the instrument itself. The desired result is thus obtained directly without intervening center points and dividers.

In this manner the odontograph becomes a general or ready made template, and equally valuable for guiding the draughtsman's right-line pen, or the pattern maker's steel scribe.

To place the instrument in position for drawing a tooth face, a table is used which should accompany the instrument. From this table a value is taken which depends upon the diameters of the pair of wheels, and the number of teeth in the wheel for which the teeth are sought. This tabular value, when multiplied by the pitch, is to be found on the graduated edge ADB, Fig. 4, of the odontograph. This done, draw the tangent DEF to the pitch line at the middle point E of a tooth ; and lay off the half thickness ED of tooth on either the tangent line or pitch line. Then place the graduated edge of the odontograph at D, and in such position that the number, and division of scale found as above, shall come precisely on the tangent line at D. Also get the curved edge, HFC, so that the curve will just lie tangent to the tangent line, as at F. Then all is ready for tracing the curve for the tooth face from the pitch line through D toward B as far as needed. By turning the instrument, which is graduated on both sides, over, and doing likewise, we get the opposite face of the same tooth. Then we have to simply draw the radial flanks when the tooth becomes fully delineated, with the exception of limiting the point and root. Clearance curves may also be struck in, if desired, as in any other case. Of course, when the setting of the instrument is once made, it may be mounted upon a rod, as, and for the purpose described above, for drawing all the teeth.

FOR INVOLUTE TEETH, ETC.

The curve which this instrument gives will closely represent initial portion of the hypocycloid, cycloid and involute, as well as the epicycloid, as far as required for a tooth face ; and hence the instrument is adapted for tracing teeth of these various forms including the rack and pinion, internal gearing and involute teeth. For the latter form of teeth the tables become very simple.

CONDITIONS OF TOOTH CURVES.

Before proceeding to the demonstrations, it will be necessary to understand how the various curves, used for tooth outlines, are conditioned.

To generate the *epicycloidal faces for teeth with radial flanks*, the generating circles, which roll upon the pitch circles, should have diameters equal to the radii of the opposite pitch lines, as set forth in Part I of this manual. Hence, as the odontograph is proposed to give nearly the epicycloid face for radial flanks, the above epicycloid is the one it should approximate to.

When one of the pitch circles is infinitely enlarged, we have the case of the *rack and pinion*, the epicycloid of the former being the cycloid generated by a circle half as large as the pinion; and its flanks are parallel to each other. Also the generating circle, whose diameter equals the radius of the rack, is infinite, and hence the generating circle for the pinion teeth is a straight line. This makes the faces of pinion teeth involutes, with the pitch circle the base of the involutes.

Therefore, for the rack and pinion with radial flanks, the faces of the rack are cycloids, and of the pinion involutes.

For the case of *involute teeth* for involute gearing in general, the base circles of the involutes are usually taken a little within the pitch circles ; the ratio of the base circles being equal to that of the pitch circles. The relation between a base circle and the pitch circle containing it is arbitrary, being generally assumed, in each case, according to the judgment of the designer, and any rule given as regulating this simply expresses the judgment of its author. The table for involute teeth is therefore adapted to suit any assumption in this regard. In this case, however, it should be borne in mind that the tangent line, used in setting the odontograph, should be drawn to these base circles instead of the pitch circles, because the involutes are normal to the base circles. But the half pitch should still be laid off on the pitch lines.

The case of *internal gearing* is peculiar, in that radial flanks for the larger wheel are impossible.* That flank which

---

* See Belanger, Cinematique, p. 121.

approaches nearest to radial, is therefore adopted, and this can be readily shown to be the involute, with the pitch circle its base. Observing that the larger wheel has its flanks outside, and faces inside the pitch circle, we see that the flanks must be generated by rolling a curve on its exterior. Rolling a circle thus, we see that the epicycloid generated rises more nearly in a radial direction, as the circle is increased in size; because the latter curve reaches the greater height. Carrying this to the limit, we have the infinite generating circle or straight line, and hence the involute curve. But suppose we adopt a rolling circle of negative curvature, as in Fig. 7, Part I. Now for this mode of generation, it is easily shown that the curve generated will be an epicycloid exactly similar and equal to that obtained by rolling a circle of positive curvature, outside the pitch circle as before, the diameter of which is equal to the difference of diameters of the generating circle of negative curvature and the pitch circle.* Hence, in either case, we get similar results, and the steepest epicycloid is the above named limiting one, viz., the involute.

The flanks of the larger wheel are therefore concave involutes. Using the same generatrix for the faces of the pinion, the latter will have involute faces.

The faces of the larger wheel will be hypocycloids, because internal, and generated by a circle whose diameter equals the radius of the pinion.

In *bevel wheels*, the pitch circles should be regarded as small circles of a sphere† which has its center situated at the point of intersection of the axes, or shafts of the wheels. These pitch circles are not, in the case of bevel wheels, the proper circles to lay out the teeth upon, but should be regarded as the bases of cones whose vertices are in the axes, outside

---

* Bour, Cours de Cinematique, p. 120: Note. Duhamel Elements de Calcule Infinitesimal.

† Willis, p. 146; Rankine, p. 144; Fairbairn, Mill and Millwork, part 2, p. 38. A. Lambert, Cinematique, Pl. 15.

the sphere, and which, developed upon a plane surface, are the desired circular arcs on which as pitch circles to delineate the teeth. The describing of teeth on these circles, being the same as on the pitch circles of spur wheels, the odontograph applies to them in the same manner, their radii number of teeth, &c., being employed in connection with the tables, instead of those of the real pitch circles.

In all these cases the same rule will apply for use of odontograph, except in involute gearing, with which we have an exception as above explained.

PARTICULAR LOGARITHMIC SPIRAL ADOPTED.

In adopting the particular logarithmic spiral for the odontograph curve, inasmuch as this curve may have an infinite variety of obliquities, it is evident that the selection is not a matter of indifference. When the obliquity, or angle between the normal and radius-vector, is very small, the arc of this spiral changes curvature less rapidly than when the obliquity is great: when the obliquity is zero, the spiral becomes a circle; and when it is 90°, the spiral is simply a radius; neither of which approximates to the epicycloid. To find that obliquity which makes the spiral best fit the epicycloid, it will probably be most satisfactory to assume an epicycloid which represents an average of those likely to be used for both curves, and adapt the spiral to it; though any ordinary logarithmic spiral will evidently conform more closely with it than the circle. The spiral which most closely osculates the epicycloid for a pair of equal pitch circles, is therefore adopted as the average spiral, because the opposite wheel may be made larger or smaller, thus making a higher or lower epicycloid. Also, it is preferable that the spiral fit for the fewest teeth, because for this the longest portion of the epicycloid would be required. The fewest number assumed is ten.

Let A F, Fig. 5, represent the pitch

line, AB the epicycloid above named, dotted beyond B, and the full line CAB,

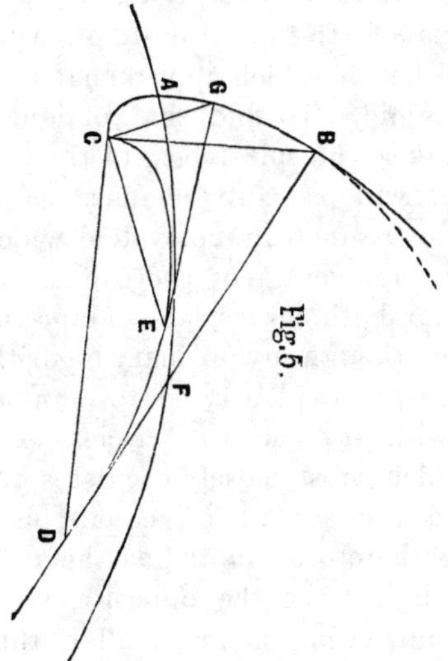

Fig. 5.

the osculating logarithmic spiral with its pole at C. Draw normals G E and B D. These normals will be common to both the epicycloid and spiral, if they closely osculate each other at A and B. Also E D will be the evolute of both. The point B is supposed to be 0.3 pitch* above the pitch line, as the ordinary height of tooth above pitch line. Or what is nearly the same, A B = 0.3 P. Also A G is assumed = 0.25 A B. Draw the normals or radii of curvature G E and B D. For the particular case under consideration we find for the epicycloid, DE= 2 GB. This fact is most conveniently proved graphically on account of the complication of the analysis. This solution was made with great care on a drawing, and it was also checked by an approximate analytical method. The results very nearly agreed, though as that by analysis was necessarily approximate, the graphical result was adopted. It happens to be also a very convenient value. The graphical operation was, in fact, partly by analysis thus: The normal to the epicycloid always coincides with the chord of the generating circle connect-

---

* In all cases in this investigation, requiring dimensions to be given to the teeth, the common and well-known rule is adopted, viz.: Thickness of tooth, $\frac{5}{11}$ P. Thickness of space, $\frac{6}{11}$ P. Height above pitch line, $\frac{3}{10}$ P. Depth below, $\frac{4}{10}$ P. See Willis, p. 113, &c.

ing the point of contingence of this and the pitch circle with the tracing point. This determines the direction of G E or B D, where B F, for instance, is a chord. The true radius of curvature B D, for an epicycloid, is $\frac{4}{3}$ B F* in the present case for radial flanks where the pitch circles are equal, or generating circle half as large as the directing pitch circle. This value of B D or G E, in terms of the chord, is from the well-known formula for the radius of curvature for epicycloids in general,† and hence the length is computed.

Now the logarithmic spiral sought must have

$$\frac{ED}{BG}=2=\text{tangent of obliquity.}$$

The evolute of the logarithmic spiral, being an equal spiral,‡ makes C E D a spiral like C A B. Also it is well known that the radii C B and C D have B C D a right angle§ when these radii vectores

* Davies and Pecks, Math. Dic., p. 222.

† See Rankine, Mach. and Millwork, p. 60, note. Redtenbacher Resultats, p. 3, rule 4. Willis, p. 142. Belanger, Cinematique, p. 103, &c.

‡ See Courtenay's Calculus, p. 181.

§ See Courtenay's Calculus, p. 173.

are drawn to the extremities of a radius of curvature BD, and similarly for ECG. This, with the second property of constant obliquity of the logarithmic spiral, makes the two triangles B C D and G C E similar. From this it follows that the triangles C B G and C D E are similar, and hence

$$CB : BG :: CD : DE,$$

or

$$\frac{DE}{BG} = \frac{CD}{BC} = \text{tangent of obliquity} = 2.$$

The equation of the logarithmic spiral is

$$\log. l = a\,\theta$$

in which a = tangent of obliquity, or $a = 2$; and therefore the logarithmic spiral sought has the equation

$$\log. l = 2\,\theta$$

or

$$l = e^{2\theta}$$

or

$$\frac{l_1}{l_2} = e^{2\,(\theta_1 - \theta_2)}$$

Values of the radius vector, l, have been carefully computed for the purpose of laying out the odontograph curve with accuracy. These were computed for the intervening angles of $22\frac{1}{2}$ degrees, which divides the circumference into sixteen equal parts; and for some of the larger values the radii subdividing these angles as follows:

For $\theta_1 - \theta_2 = 22\frac{1}{2}^\circ \quad \frac{l_1}{l_2} = 2.1933$

$\theta =$	θ_1	l_1	$= 0.5000$
" $= \theta_1 +$	$22\frac{1}{2}^\circ$	l_2	$= 1.0966$
" $= \theta_1 +$	45°	l_3	$= 2.4052$
" $= \theta_1 +$	$67\frac{1}{2}^\circ$	l_4	$= 5.2753$
" $= \theta_1 +$	90°	l_5	$= 11.5700$
" $= \theta_1 +$	$101\frac{1}{4}^\circ$	$l_{5\frac{1}{2}}$	$= 17.1350$
" $= \theta_1 +$	$112\frac{1}{2}^\circ$	l_6	$= 25.3700$
" $= \theta_1 +$	$123\frac{3}{4}^\circ$	$l_{6\frac{1}{2}}$	$= 37.5820$
" $= \theta_1 +$	135°	l_7	$= 55.6560$

With these values, the odontograph, as shown in Fig. 4, was laid out, not only the curve A D B, but C F H; these being similar and equal as above explained. From the fact that tangent obliquity = 2, we may, when a radius l is laid off for a point on A D B, draw a line at right angles, and lay off on it $2\,l$, which will give a point on C F H.

EQUATION OF THE ODONTOGRAPH CURVE.

In the analytical demonstration of the applicability of this curve, an equation will be needed for it, which can be combined with those for the curves which are proposed for the outlines of teeth. For reasons which will appear hereafter, an equation is required which gives the relation between the abscissas $a\,e$ and the ordinates $e\,b$, Fig. 6. Let $a\,c$ be the radius of curvature of the spiral at a. Let fall upon this a perpendicular $b\,e$. Also prolong $a\,c$ to d. Some point d can always be found with which, as a center, a circle may be struck through a and b. Now let us propose that $c\,d = q \times e\,b$ as a relation sufficiently exact for any possible height of tooth, $e\,b$, above pitch line.

Then we will have from the property of the circle,

$$a\,e\,(2\,a\,d - a\,e) = \overline{e\,b}^2,$$

or calling $a\,e = y$ and $e\,b = x$, $a\,c = \tau$, we have

$$y\,[2\,(\tau + q\,x) - y] = x^2$$

whence

$$\tau = \frac{x}{2}\left\{\frac{x}{y} + \frac{y}{x} - 2q\right\} \quad . \quad . \qquad (1)$$

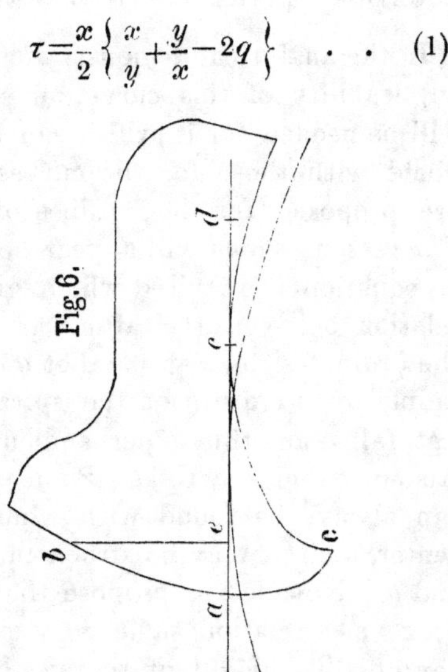
Fig. 6.

If, in this equation, q proves to be constant, we have the equation desired. To this end the following results have been very carefully determined graphically, this method being the only one admissible for complexity of formulas:

For $r=2.0$ inch $x=1.1$ inch $q=.596$
$r=2.0$ inch $x=2.0$ inch $q=.588$
$r=4.4$ inch $x=1.0$ inch $q=.561$
$r=4.4$ inch $x=2.5$ inch $q=.557$
$r=4.4$ inch $x=4.5$ inch $q=.562$
$r=9.0$ inch $x=0.5$ inch $q=.595$
$r=9.0$ inch $x=9.0$ inch $q=.599$
$r=9.5$ inch $x=2.2$ inch $q=.555$
$r=9.5$ inch $x=5.5$ inch $q=.600$

Mean . . $q=.579$

These figures show that q is very nearly constant; in fact, the differences can only be accounted for as errors of the graphical operation; errors which might be expected for the reason that the point d, Fig. 6, may vary its position considerably, and yet cause but slight variations at b. We may therefore adopt this, not only as constant, but as the correct value of q for the particular spiral chosen, and this value was employed in the formulas when computing the tables for the odontograph. Equation (1) is entirely empirical, and will not apply to the spiral for a very great range; though to an extent greater than ever needed for the present purpose, it is practically exact. It is necessary to resort to the empirical method, because the equation of this spiral cannot be expressed in rectangular co-ordinates.

DEMONSTRATION FOR EPICYCLOIDAL SPUR GEARING.

To show that the odontograph, as above proposed, is applicable to the case of ordinary epicycloidal gearing-teeth with radial flanks, it will be necessary to prove that the value of r to be found on the scale by which the instrument is set, can be computed when certain functional parts of the gears in question are known ; and also, to show that it can be expressed in so few terms, that values of it may be computed beforehand, and arranged in tabular form, it will be necessary to resort to mathematical expressions for r, by which it can be discussed, and by which we may determine the number of quantities required to express it. For instance, if it can be expressed in terms of two different quantities only, one table will suffice for all values of τ. But if it requires three quantities for its expression, a series of tables will be necessary.

By aid of the equations of the epicycloid the above co-ordinates x and y may be expressed in quantities belonging to the wheels.

Let R=the radius of the pitch circle of the wheel for which the teeth are sought, whether it be the larger or smaller.

Let N=the number of its teeth.

Let r=the radius of the wheel which is to work with the wheel sought, and equal to the diameter of the rolling circle for generating the faces sought.

Let n=the number of its teeth.

Let P=the pitch of the teeth$=\frac{2\,\pi\,R}{N}$ $=\frac{2\,\pi\,r}{n}$.

Let τ=the radius of curvature of the curve of odontograph, as above, the numerical value of which is also the number to be used for setting the instrument, also the tabular numbers.

Let x and y=co-ordinates as in equation (1) of odontograph curve above, x=0.3 P.

Let θ=an angle, which may be considered as an auxiliary quantity, simply; or as the angle which locates the center of the rolling circle.

Then the well-known * polar equation of the epicycloid is—

$$(\text{rad.vector})^2=(R+x)^2=R^2+r\left\{R+\frac{r}{2}\right\}\left\{1-\cos.\frac{2R}{r}\theta\right\}$$

whence

$$\cos.\frac{2R}{r}\theta=1-\frac{\left\{1+\frac{x}{R}\right\}^2-1}{\frac{r}{R}\left\{1+\frac{r}{2R}\right\}}$$

* See Price's Calculus, vol. i, p. 349.

or

$$\cos.\frac{2\,\mathrm{N}}{n}\theta=1-\frac{\left\{1+\frac{0.3\,\mathrm{P}}{\mathrm{R}}\right\}^{2}-1}{\frac{n}{\mathrm{N}}\left\{1+\frac{n}{2\,\mathrm{N}}\right\}} \qquad (2)$$

This value of θ is in terms of the two quantities $\frac{\mathrm{P}}{\mathrm{R}}$ and $\frac{n}{\mathrm{N}}$ only, as desired.

The polar equation is here employed instead of that referred to rectangular co-ordinates, because the former is resolvable with respect to θ, and the latter not. The latter, however, would have been preferable to the extent of about the difference between the height of b, Fig. 6, above the tangent and above the pitch line, because $b\ e$, which is about midway between a, and the middle of the tooth, is almost exactly equal to x as given by the rectangular equation. But this difference is very small in wheels of the fewest teeth, say 8 or 10, and inappreciable in larger wheels.

An expression for y is most readily obtained by employing the well-known *

* See Price's Calculus, vol. i, p. 283.

equation of y in terms of θ for rectangular co-ordinates to the epicycloid.

In Fig. 7, let A B represent the face of the tooth for the wheel whose center

Fig. 7.

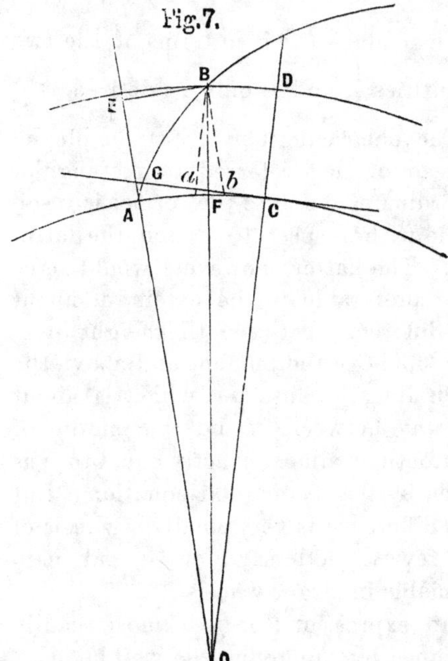

is O. Take C D the height of the tooth above the pitch line reckoned on the center line of tooth, and $= \mathrm{B\,F} = 0.3\ \mathrm{P}$, nearly $= x$. Let C G represent the tangent to the pitch line at the center point C of tooth, as above described.

Now, since the co-ordinates x and y in equation (1) of the odontograph curve represent the height of B above the tangent C G, and the distance from the face along the tangent C G to the perpendicular let fall from B upon C G respectively, or equal to B F and A a respectively, very nearly, we have to find, by help of the equation of the epicycloid, between y and θ, the value of A a. But this equation gives E B, or A b. Drawing B b parallel to A E, and B a parallel to D C, we have

$$ab : \mathrm{F\,B} :: \mathrm{A\,C} : \mathrm{C\,O}$$

or

$$ab : x :: \tfrac{5}{22}\,\mathrm{P} : \mathrm{R}$$

since the thickness of tooth$=\frac{5}{11}$ P.

Hence

$$ab=\frac{5}{22}\,\frac{x\,\mathrm{P}}{\mathrm{R}}=\frac{5}{22}\,\frac{0.3\ \mathrm{P}^2}{\mathrm{R}}=\frac{\mathrm{P}^2}{\mathrm{R}}0.06819$$

and hence, by aid of the equation of the epicycloid,

$$A\,a = y = E\,B - a\,b = \left(R + \frac{r}{2}\right) \sin.\,\theta - \frac{r}{2} \sin.\left(\frac{2\,N}{n} + 1\right)\theta - a\,b$$

or

$$\frac{y}{P} = \frac{R}{2\,P}\frac{n}{N}\left\{\left(\frac{2\,N}{n} + 1\right) \sin.\,\theta - \sin.\left(\frac{2\,N}{n} + 1\right)\theta\right\} - \frac{P}{R}0.06819 \quad (3)$$

This equation, together with (2), enables us to compute $\frac{y}{P}$ when $\frac{P}{R}$ and $\frac{n}{N}$ only, are known, θ being eliminated between (2) and (3).

Observing that $x = 0.3$ P, equation (1) may be written

$$\frac{\tau}{P} = 0.15\left(\frac{.3\,P}{y} + \frac{y}{0.3\,P} - 2q\right) \quad . \quad (4)$$

So that $\frac{\tau}{P}$ becomes fully known when the two quantities $\frac{P}{R}$ and $\frac{n}{N}$ belonging to the pair of wheels under consideration become known. Or, observing that $\frac{P}{R} = \frac{2\,\pi}{N}$, the most convenient forms of the equations for computation are

$$\cos. \frac{2\,N}{n}\,\theta = 1 - \frac{\left(1 + \frac{1.885}{N}\right)^2 - 1}{\frac{n}{N}\left(1 + \frac{n}{2\,N}\right)} \quad . \quad (5)$$

$$\frac{y}{P} = 0.07958\ N \frac{n}{N} \left\{ \left(\frac{2\,N}{n} + 1\right) \sin.\theta - \sin. \left(\frac{2\,N}{n} + 1\right)\theta \right\} - \frac{0.42841}{N} \quad . \quad . \quad (6)$$

$$\frac{\tau}{P} = 0.15\left(\frac{0.3\,P}{y} + \frac{y}{0.3\,P} - 1.158\right) \quad . \quad (7)$$

These formulas enable us to compute $\frac{\tau}{P}$ when $\frac{N}{n}$ and N are known. Table I contains most of the values $\frac{\tau}{P}$ needed in practice, and obtained from these formulas. The tabular value of $\frac{\tau}{P}$, when multiplied by P gives τ the index number for setting the odontograph. Examples will be given hereafter, illustrating the use of the instrument and table in delineating gear teeth.

DEMONSTRATION FOR THE RACK AND PINION.

For this case formula (6) becomes indeterminate, and hence fails. It will, therefore, be necessary to deduce others.

The cycloid for the tooth faces on the rack, flanks radial, will have the following values of x and y * :

$$x=\frac{r}{2}\left(1-\cos.\ \theta\right)$$

$$y=\frac{r}{2}\left(\theta-\sin.\ \theta\right)$$

and hence

$$\cos.\ \theta=1-\frac{1.2\ \pi}{n}\quad .\ .\ .\quad (8)$$

$$\frac{y}{r}=\frac{n}{4\ \pi}\left(\theta-\sin.\ \theta\right)\quad .\quad (9)$$

By expanding cos. θ into a series and dropping all after θ^2, by which we involve an error of only $\frac{1}{28}$ part for the case of 8 teeth, and much less for a greater number; and similarly expanding sin. θ into a series, omitting the

* Price's Calculus, vol. i, p. 280.

terms following θ^3 with an opposite error of $\frac{1}{50}$ for 8 teeth, giving a residual error of about $\frac{1}{50}$ we may write,

$$\frac{y}{\mathrm{P}}=\frac{1}{10}\sqrt{\frac{2.4\,\pi}{n}} \quad . \quad . \quad (10)$$

This, combined with (7), was used for computing the tabular values for racks given at the bottom of table I.

For the involute faces of the pinion we readily obtain special formulas.

Let A H, Fig. 8, be regarded as the

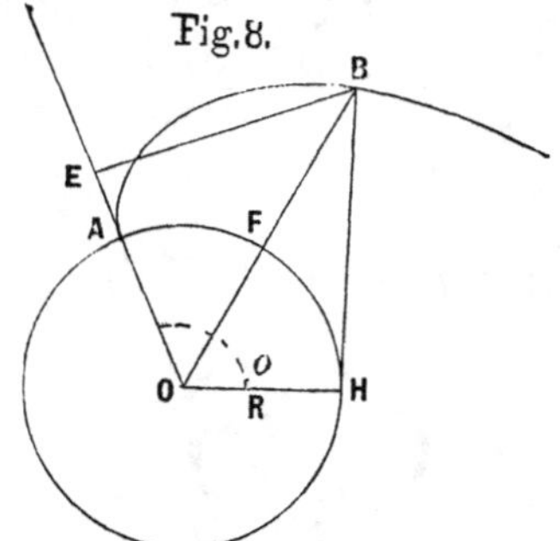

pitch line, AB as a tooth face of the involute form, and B F height of tooth above the pitch line and equal to 0.3 P $= x$. We will have $a\ b$ same as before.

$$\therefore \quad y = \text{E B} - a\,b$$

as in Fig. 8.

$$\text{E B} = (\text{R} + \text{B F}) \text{ arc B O E nearly}$$

$$= (\text{R} + 0.3 \text{ P}) (\theta - \text{B O H})$$

$$\text{H B} = \text{A F H} = \text{R}\,\theta = \text{R tang. B O H}$$

Hence

$$y = \text{E B} - a\,b = (\text{R} + 0.3 \text{ P}) (\theta - \text{tang.}^{-1} \theta) - a\,b$$

or

$$\frac{y}{\text{P}} = \left(\frac{\text{N}}{2\,\pi} + 0.3\right) \left(\theta - \text{tang.}^{-1} \theta\right) - \frac{0.42841}{\text{N}} \quad . \quad (11)$$

and

$$\overline{\text{B H}}^2 = \overline{\text{R}\,\theta}^2 = (\text{R} + 0.3 \text{ P})^2 - \text{R}^2$$

or

$$\theta^2 = \left(1 - \frac{0.6\,\pi}{\text{N}}\right)^2 - 1 \quad . \quad (12)$$

which equations, combined with (7), were used in bringing out the tabular quantities marked "Pinion" near the bottom of table I.

It is observed that we have one line of values only for each, the rack and pinion, the reason for this is that the value of $\frac{\tau}{P}$ for the rack and pinion become known in terms of one arbitrary quantity instead of two.

DEMONSTRATION FOR WHEELS WITH INVOLUTE TEETH.

Having a set of values of $\frac{\tau}{P}$ for involute faces, we are at once prepared to lay out any involute gear-teeth with the odontograph, from the fact that in this form of teeth each wheel is independent of all others. In this case, however, we must observe that the tangent line E D, Fig. 4, should be drawn to the base circle instead of from the pitch circle, as stated above under *conditions* for involute teeth. The half thickness of tooth should still be laid off on the pitch line, because this is the proper line to reckon tooth thicknesses on. The tabular values of Table II are therefore the same as those for *Pinion*, Table I.

DEMONSTRATION FOR WHEELS IN INTERNAL GEAR.

First consider the larger wheel, in which the faces are internal and hence hypocycloids. Equations (2) and (3) apply to this case by changing the signs of r and x, and hence

$$\cos. \frac{2\,R}{r}\,\theta = 1 - \frac{1 - \left(1 - \frac{x}{R}\right)^2}{\frac{r}{R}\left(1 - \frac{r}{2\,R}\right)}$$

or

$$\cos. \frac{2\,N}{n}\,\theta = 1 - \frac{1 - \left(1 - \frac{0.6\,\pi}{N}\right)^2}{\frac{n}{N}\left(1 - \frac{n}{2\,N}\right)} \quad (13)$$

and

$$\frac{y}{P} = \frac{R}{2\,P}\,\frac{n}{N}\left\{\left(\frac{2\,N}{n} - 1\right)\sin.\,\theta - \sin.\left(\frac{2\,N}{n} - 1\right)\theta\right\} + \frac{0.6\,\pi}{N}\,0.2273 \quad (14)$$

which, combined with (7), were used in producing the first part of table III. The flanks of the pinion are supposed to be radial, and those of the wheel involutes as set forth under *conditions* for these wheels. The external involute flanks of the wheel are laid out by aid of the values given in table I for "*pinion*," the tangent line E D, Fig. 4, being drawn to the pitch line from the middle of a *space*, to suit the present reversed conditions from outside to inside.

The faces of the pinion, being also *involutes*, the same set of tabular values last-named apply, which for convenience's sake are arranged in the latter part of Table III.

CASE OF BEVEL WHEELS.

Observing the explanations, page 76, regarding bevel wheels, either epicycloidal or involute teeth may be laid out for these wheels.

Table I.

FOR EPICYCLOID TEETH WITH RADIAL FLANKS.

Values of $\frac{\tau}{P}$ *in inches:* or, number by which to multiply the pitch, measured in *inches*, to obtain the index number for setting the odontograph.

$\frac{R}{r}$ or $\frac{r}{R}$ Radius of wheel sought, Divided by Radius of other wheel.	Number of teeth in wheel for which the teeth are sought, N and n.												
	8	16	24	32	40	48	56	64	72	80	88	96	112
$\frac{1}{12}$ = .083	.321	.458	.555										
$\frac{1}{6}$ = .167	.317	.450	.551	.634	.704								
$\frac{1}{4}$ = .250	.311	.438	.540	.624	.692	.780	.853						
$\frac{1}{3}$ = .333	.300	.426	.526	.611	.679	.770	.831	.869	.910	.965	1.017	1.080	1.225
$\frac{5}{12}$ = .417	.293	.417	.515	.598	.666	.741	.808	.853	.894	.948	1.000	1.052	1.147
$\frac{1}{2}$ = .500	.283	.406	.504	.584	.654	.722	.786	.834	.878	.930	.980	1.032	1.132
$\frac{7}{12}$ = .583	.272	.394	.492	.573	.640	.705	.766	.817	.862	.911	.960	.995	1.107

$\frac{2}{3}$=.667	.266	.382	.479	.558	.627	.690	.748	.799	.845	.895	.946	.987	1.089
$\frac{3}{4}$=.750	.252	.369	.467	.545	.613	.677	.733	.784	.834	.878	.923	.973	1.066
$\frac{5}{6}$=.833	.245	.379	.456	.534	.602	.662	.721	.768	.820	.862	.905	.957	1.047
$\frac{11}{12}$=.917	.238	.348	.446	.522	.590	.648	.709	.754	.806	.847	.892	.938	1.037
1.	.230	.338	.435	.510	.577	.634	.693	.740	.791	.832	.876	.919	1.007
$\frac{12}{11}$=1.09	.221	.329	.423	.500	.563	.621	.679	.722	.774	.813	.856	.898	.990
$\frac{6}{5}$=1.20	.211	.318	.411	.489	.548	.607	.661	.705	.755	.794	.836	.877	.968
$\frac{4}{3}$=1.33	.202	.307	.396	.472	.532	.590	.640	.685	.731	.771	.812	.855	.935
$\frac{3}{2}$=1.50	.193	.294	.381	.452	.511	.571	.618	.663	.707	.727	.789	.827	.896
$\frac{12}{7}$=1.71	.183	.278	.362	.428	.487	.542	.591	.636	.678	.716	.756	.794	.848
2	.174	.260	.336	.400	.458	.511	.560	.604	.642	.679	.715	.748	.795
$\frac{12}{5}$=2.40		.219	.304	.362	.421	.474	.523	.562	.597	.633	.663	.693	.739
3			.265	.321	.379	.428	.473	.508	.540	.572	.600	.624	.673
4				.271	.328	.374	.409	.435	.467	.491	.521	.548	.600
6					.254	.289	.321	.348	.372	.397	.428	.460	.519
12								.257	.292	.286	.318	.361	.417

For both Rack and Pinion, use number of teeth in *pinion* for N, above.

Rack...	.338	.513	.657	.777	.884	.982	1.071	1.155	1.233	1.304	1.378	1.444	1.573
Pinion..	.323	.443	.551	.642	.718	.785	.847	.897	.941	.990	1.032	1.067	1.122

Table II.

FOR INVOLUTE TEETH.

Values of $\frac{\tau}{P}$ *in inches*: or, number by which to multiply the pitch, measured in inches, to obtain the index number for setting the odontograph.

Number of teeth in wheel: or N and *n*.												
8	16	24	32	40	48	56	64	72	80	88	96	112
.323	.443	.551	.642	.718	.785	.847	.897	.941	.990	1.032	1.067	1.122

N. B.—The tangent should be drawn to the base circles.

EXAMPLES.

To show the application of the tables, the following examples are given: Let the pair of wheels be the same for each example, the teeth simply being different; let the number of teeth in the smaller wheel be 16 and in the larger 56. Also take the same pitch for all, and equal to two inches.

1st. For *epicycloidal teeth* with radial flanks. For this we must use table I, which requires the ratio of the radii of the wheels; or, what is the same thing, the ratio of the number of teeth in the wheels.

For the larger wheel the required ratio is

$$\frac{R}{r}=3\tfrac{1}{2} \text{ and } N=56.$$

Running down the column headed "$\frac{R}{r}$" we find $3\frac{1}{2}$ comes midway between 3 and 4; and opposite them, under "56," corresponding to N, the numbers .473 and .409. Taking the mean for the interpolated value, we have .441 as the multiplier for the pitch. Hence

$$.441 \times 2 \text{ inches pitch} = .882 \text{ inches},$$

which is the index number, or the number to look out on the scale A D B, Fig. 4, which point must be brought to coincide with the tangent D E. Then, placing the curve C F tangent to the tangent line as shown in the figure, the tooth face curve may be drawn.

For the smaller wheel we have

$$\frac{r}{R} = .286+, \text{ and } n = 16.$$

Running down the column headed "$\frac{r}{R}$" we find no ratio = .286, but .250 and .333. Interpolating by the well-known method of proportional parts, we find, in column headed "16," for the multiplier the number .433. Hence

$$.433 \times 2 = .866 \text{ inches}.$$

which is the setting or index number required for the small wheel.

2d. For the *rack*, suppose the large wheel is made infinite and the pitch line straight. Then the pinion will have 16 teeth, and the multiplier is .513. Hence

$$.513 \times 2 = 1.023 \text{ inches,}$$

which is the index number for setting the odontograph to the straight line of the rack.

For the *pinion*, we find the multiplier to be .443. Hence

$$.443 \times 2 = .886 \text{ inches,}$$

which is the required number for the pinion.

3d. For the case of *involute teeth*, the multiplier for the larger wheel is .847, table II, and for the smaller it is .443, by aid of which the odontograph is set a tangent to the base circle as above explained.

4th. For the case of internal gearing we have, for obtaining the external involute flanks,

$$\frac{R}{r} = 3\tfrac{1}{2}, \text{ and } N = 56.$$

Not finding 56 in the line of numbers of teeth, table III, we interpolate between 40 and 60 for the ratio 3. This gives for N = 56 the multiplier .649. Similarly for ratio 4, we find multiplier .490. Taking the mean of these for the ratio $3\frac{1}{2}$, and we get .569 as the desired multiplier. Hence

$$.569 \times 2 \text{ inches pitch} = 1.138 \text{ inches.}$$

for the index number.

For the faces of the wheel we find, from the lower line of table III, .841 as the required multiplier, and 1.682 as the index number.

To set the odontograph. Observing the foot-note of table III, the tangent line E D, Fig. 4, to which the instrument is set, is drawn from the middle of the space, as though the space in this case, outside the pitch line, were a tooth.

For the faces of the pinion teeth the multiplier is .443, as in lower line of table III, &c., &c.

TABLE III.

FOR INTERNAL GEARING, PINION FLANKS RADIAL.

Values of $\frac{r}{P}$ *in inches:* or, number by which to multiply the pitch, measured in inches, to obtain the index number for setting the odontograph.

$\frac{R}{r}$ or Radius of wheel. Divided by Radius of pinion.	Wheel: Number of teeth, or N.						
	8	16	24	40	60	100	150
2	*Faces*	.400	.556	.818	1.082	1.514	1.887
3		.210	.317	.497	.687	1.017	1.322
4			.232	.370	.520	.767	1.027
6				.268	.387	.555	.687
12					.282	.387	.447
Flanks of wheel and *faces* of pinion.							
	.323	.443	.551	.718	.872	1.084	1.270

N. B.—In laying out the *flanks* for the *wheel*, the tangent should be drawn from the center of the space, and not center of tooth.

CASE OF CHANGE WHEELS, AND "SETS" OF EPICYCLOIDAL GEARING.

The demonstrations for, and the applications of, the new odontograph have, thus far, proceeded upon the supposition that the flanks of the teeth laid out are radial. Though this form is the most convenient to delineate, and possesses greatest freedom in action as shown in Part I, yet some may prefer to construct wheels so that all, having a given pitch, may be used in any interchangeable manner; or, it may be desired in a pair of gears that the teeth have thick bases, such as obtained by using small generating circles, describing curved hypocycloidal flanks.

The preceding demonstrations and tables cover this case. The equations may have $\frac{N}{n}$ replaced by $\frac{R}{r}$, in which r has been regarded as the radius of the wheel gearing with the one sought, and equal to the diameter of the generating circle. But we readily see that it is only necessary to consider r as the diameter of the generating circle in all cases, due regard being given only to using the same value of r in laying out the other wheel, outside of one and inside the other, and conversely; or, for a given "set," the same throughout, as pointed out in Part I.

The new odontograph is therefore of universal application in epicycloidal gearing, giving any such flare, and thickness of tooth base, as may be demanded by the most fastidious draughtsman.

For describing the faces of the teeth now considered Table I is sufficient, the *diameter* of the generating circle always forming the denominator of the fraction $\frac{R}{r}$. For the flanks, the first part of Table III would apply, though with less approximative results than those obtained by aid of the latter part of Table IV, prepared expressly for this.

The odontograph is found to osculate best with the hypocycloid when it is located by aid of a tangent line E D, Fig. 4, drawn from A, instead of E; or, from the sides instead of middle of tooth; and hence, to lay out flanks other than radial, draw tangents to the pitch line at each side of the tooth, and on them, locate the instrument by aid of second part of Table IV, as on any other tangent, observing that the back edge of the odontograph should now be turned toward the center of the wheel, instead of from it, as in drawing faces.

This portion of this table was computed by aid of equations (13), (14) and (7), after suppressing the last term of (14); which term, it is seen, is *a b*, Fig. 7, now made zero by reducing A C, Fig. 7, to zero, as above explained.

From the fact that the curve C D B, and C F H, Fig. 4, are one and the same, except as to length, the instrument may, if preferred, be located by a radius instead of a tangent line. Suppose, for instance, D F, be a radius, drawn at one side of a tooth, with the pitch line intersecting it at F. By laying off F D, outward from the circle, and equal, in inches, to the proper index number, then F H, when the instrument is properly located is the required flank.

For this mode of locating the instrument the index number obtained from the table should be divided by two, because always 2 C D=C F.

EXAMPLE.

Take number of teeth 16 and 56, and pitch 2 inches, as in previous examples, and a four-inch generating circle. The pitch circle radii are 5.1 and 17.8 inches, and hence, for wheel, "radius of wheel sought divided by *diameter* of describing circle" = 4.45. For this, and for N = 56, TABLE IV, referring to TABLE I, gives .39, which, multiplied by pitch, gives .78, the index number for wheel faces.

Interpolating in TABLE IV the numbers 4.45 and 56 give .52, and multiplied by pitch 1.04, for the index number for the wheel flanks. Similarly, for the pinion, we get the index numbers .628 and 2.90.

Table IV.

FOR UNIVERSAL APPLICATION OF NEW ODONTOGRAPH FOR EPICYCLOIDAL GEARING.

Values of $\frac{\tau}{P}$ *in inches,* or, nnmber by which to multiply the pitch, measured in inches, to obtain the index number for setting the odontograph.

Radius of Wheel sought divided by *diamete* of describing circle.	Number of teeth, N, in the Wheel sought.						
	8	16	24	40	60	100	150
	For Faces.						

Values same as in Table I.

	For Flanks.						
1.5	.775	1.177	1.540	1.958	2.607	3.229	3.875
2	.440	.632	.805	1.094	1.391	1.786	2.217
3			.454	.650	.860	1.190	1.585
4			.276	.410	.592	.836	1.126
6			.200	.324	.440	.603	.724
12					.322	.417	.470

N. B.—For the *faces* the tangent D E, Fig. 4, should be drawn from the middle of a tooth ; and for the *flanks* the tangent should be drawn from the sides of a tooth.

MODIFIED FORM OF THE WILLIS ODONTOGRAPH.

The odontograph now under consideration is termed a modified form of the Willis odontograph, not because it bears any resemblance to the Willis odontograph, but because it is based upon the theory of Prof. Willis for the forming of teeth of wheels by circle arcs, and also because it gives centers to tooth arcs as does the Willis odontograph, instead of forming in itself a template for the curves.

By constructing the instrument so that it can be set to various angles, instead of being fixed at 75° ; and by preparing suitable tables to accompany it, we may be able with it to lay out teeth with straight flanks for all wheels, the faces of the teeth being circular arcs whose centers are given by the instrument.

The analysis by which these facts are demonstrated is essentially that of Prof. Willis, and given in his *Principles of Mechanism*, 2d ed., pp. 132, 136.

According to the Willis theory for forming each tooth with four circular arcs, whose centers are on the line of action, if certain centers be removed to an infinite distance, the arcs struck from such centers will be straight lines, perpendicular to the line of action. This is supposed to be done in the present case for the flank arcs, and when the line of action is suitably inclined, these perpendiculars become radii on the pinion and inclined lines on the wheel.

With these conditions imposed at the outset, the analysis becomes extremely simple, as follows: In Fig. 9 let A and B represent the pitch circles, C the pitch point, and E F the line of action. Draw A E and B F perpendicular to E F as shown. Let α = angle C A E = C B F, A C = R, B C = r, and C G = D. Now Prof. Willis' diagram, p. 135, becomes Fig. 9 when A k and B K are made parallel to line of action as in Fig. 9. I will simply explain Fig. 9, referring those who wish to study the diagram further to Prof. Willis' book. G is a center for describing a tooth face of A, and H a center for a face of a tooth of

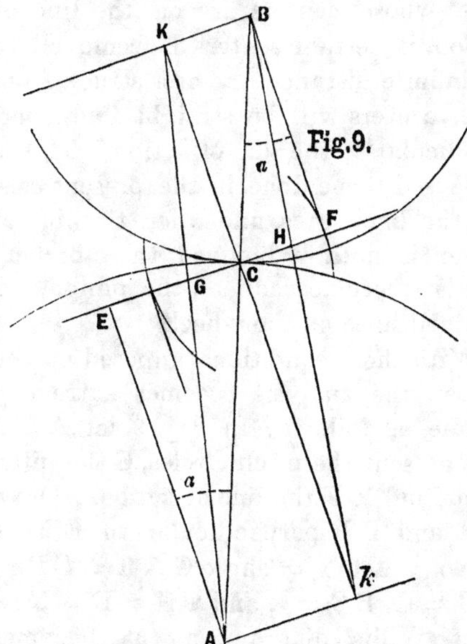

B. The center for the flank against which the face, struck from G, works, being on B K at an infinite distance, the flank is perpendicular to E F. The point serving as the origin for this face

and flank may be assumed at any position* on the line E F, but should generally be not far from F, and for radial flanks for B, must be at F. Similarly for E if the flanks for E are to be radial.

To render the odontograph convenient in practical use, and to keep the radii of the tooth faces within reasonable limits for all cases, such as when the pair of wheels are of equal size and also of very different sizes, it is found advisable to make the flanks of the smaller of the pair of wheels or pinion radial in all cases; and for the larger wheel, of such inclination that the same radius for the tooth faces of the wheel will be right for the pinion. To this end C F is taken, arbitrarily equal to one-third of the pitch, so that the radius of the faces for both wheels is G F = G C + $\frac{1}{3}$ pitch. The point G is given by the odontograph and it is easy to lay off a third of the pitch C F. Then we will have, C F B being always preserved a right angle,

---

* This fact is pointed out by Prof. Willis.

$$C F=\frac{P}{3}=r \sin. \propto$$

$$\therefore \sin. \propto=\frac{P}{3 r}=\frac{2 \pi}{3 n}$$

where n=number of teeth in pinion.

Again

$$C F : C H :: R+r : R$$

$$C H=D=C F \frac{R}{R+r}=\frac{R}{R+r} \cdot \frac{P}{3}$$

But

$$C F : C E :: r : R$$

and

$$C G : C E :: r : R+r$$

$$\therefore C G=C E \frac{r}{R+r}=C F \frac{r}{R+r} \frac{R}{r}=\frac{R}{R+r} \cdot \frac{P}{3}$$

or

$$C G=C H.$$

This shows that it is only necessary to set the odontograph once to obtain either C G or C H. Taking the distance from C to the origin of tooth arcs the same for both wheels gives equal radii for the faces of both wheels, and the arcs and flanks are easily struck in as shown in Fig. 9. To draw all other arcs the centers may be found, which lie in circles concentric with the pitch lines. The drawing of the non-radial flanks of A will require a little attention that they be drawn at the proper angle with the radius, or rather simply perpendicular to E F at the proper point.

The quantities α and $\frac{D}{P}$ are given in terms of n and $\frac{R}{r}$, respectively, in the following table for a number of values, which will aid in the practical use of the instrument, the necessary setting values being thus obtained beforehand. When the data fall between values in the table, interpolations will be necessary, though readily made.

THE INSTRUMENT, AND MODE OF USING IT.

The modified odontograph is shown full size in Fig. 10, with its scales, &c.,

ready for use, in delineating teeth of six inches pitch.

Table V.

FOR THE MODIFIED WILLIS ODONTOGRAPH.

Values of the setting angle α, *and of* $\frac{D}{P}$ *for position of arc center*, for tooth face for radial flanks for *pinion* and for inclined flanks for the wheel.

Number of teeth in pinion, $=n$.	Setting angle for odontograph, $=\alpha$		Larger radius divided by smaller, $=\frac{R}{r}$	Tooth center distance divided by pitch, $=\frac{D}{P}$
	Deg.	Min.		
10	12	05	1	.167
15	8	02	1.5	.200
20	6	01	2	.222
30	4	00	3	.250
40	3	00	4	.267
60	2	00	5	.278
80	1	30	6	.286
100	1	12	7	.292
130	0	55	8	.296
160	0	45	9	.300
200	0	36	10	.303
260	0	28	11	.306
300	0	24	12	.308

N. B.—The two parts of this table are entirely independent of each other, the first giving the setting angle α, without regard to where the line is in second part of table giving $\frac{D}{P}$.

In using the instrument the point C is to be brought to the pitch point C, Fig. 9. Then the angle α obtained from the table is to be looked out on the sectoral scale A B, and that point placed upon the radius A C, Fig. 9. The instrument is then in position. A line should then be drawn along E C and produced in the direction of F, perpendicular to which the flanks are to be drawn. Then the distance D, obtained by multiplying $\frac{D}{P}$ of the last table by P, is to be set off on the scale C E, Fig. 10, which point is the center G, Fig. 9, from which to strike the tooth face. Then C F, equal $\frac{1}{3}$ P as explained above, is set off on line E F as the origin of a tooth face and flank as shown in Fig. 9. We then have the length G F for the radius

Fig. 10.

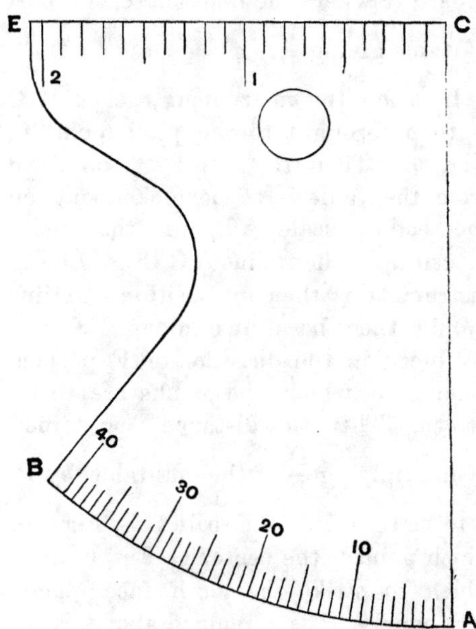

Modified Willis Odontograph.

Full size.

of a face of A, which is also the radius for a face of B to be used at the centers H and G respectively. The flanks are per pendicular to E F and tangent to the tooth arcs as shown, and each face works with its tangent flank, as shown in Fig. 9. By repeating these faces and flanks the teeth become fully drawn, as in Fig. 13. The flanks of the smaller wheel are always radial, but those of the larger wheel never, except in case both wheels become equal, when the flanks of both are radial.

It will hardly be necessary to follow this description with an example.

ODONTOGRAPH TEETH COMPARED.

Fig. 11 is an accurate drawing of a part of the teeth of a pair of wheels as laid out by the well known *Willis Odontograph.*

Fig. 12 is likewise a carefully executed drawing of a portion of the same pair of gears as laid out by the *New Odontograph.*

Fig. 13 shows the form of teeth of the

same pair of wheels as laid out by the *Modified Willis Instrument.*

The smaller of the wheels has twelve teeth, and the larger has 144 teeth.

These drawings will enable the reader to form a very correct opinion as to the relative merits of the results of the three instruments. This is not difficult to such as are familiar with the proper form of gear teeth. While this may be true, still it remains doubtful which to adopt for practical use. Such doubts however may be removed on taking a direct comparative view of the respective difficulties, and conveniences of application of the three instruments, which, for the purpose of furthering this object is given below.

PRACTICE WITH THE THREE ODONTOGRAPHS COMPARED.

The well known *Willis Odontograph,* in laying out one side of a tooth requires: 1st, that the pitch be laid off on the pitch line; 2d, that this pitch be bisected to obtain the origin of arcs ; 3d, that a radius be drawn at one end of the pitch and the instrument placed on it ; 4th, a quantity taken from a table by which the center point is found on the odontograph scale and point noted on drawing ; 5th, that a radius be drawn at the other end of the pitch, and the instrument placed on it ; 6th, a second quantity taken from the table by which a second center point is found and noted on drawing for a second arc center ; 7th, that a pair of dividers be placed at one center, the face or flank struck ; 8th, that similarly a flank or face be struck from the second center ; 9th, and finally that caution be exercised to point off the right center at the two settings of instrument, and also that the proper part, flank or face, be drawn from the centers.

The *New Odontograph* in laying out the side of a tooth requires : 1st, that a tangent line be drawn to the pitch circle; 2d, that the half thickness of tooth be laid off from the point of tangency ; 3d, a quantity looked out from a table ; 4th, that this be multiplied by the pitch by which the instrument is properly set on the tangent line; 5th, that a scribe be drawn along edge of instrument for the *face;* 6th, and lastly, that a radial flank be drawn from the intersection of face with the pitch line.

The *Modified Willis Odontograph* requires : 1st, that a radius be drawn ; 2d, that a setting angle be found from a table by which the instrument is set ; 3d, that a second quantity be taken from a table ; 4th, that this quantity be multiplied by the pitch, by which the center point for the face is found and noted ; 5th, that a line be drawn along the edge of the odontograph, perpendicular to which the flank is afterwards drawn ; 6th, that the one-third pitch be laid off from the end of the radius upon which the instrument was set ; 7th, that by aid of a pair of dividers the face arc be struck ; 8th, and finally, that the flank be drawn perpendicular to the line traced for the purpose, as above described.

COMPARATIVE VIEW OF THE INSTRUMENTS AND TABLES.

As to the tables for the three instruments, those for the modified Willis odontograph are the most compact of all, having only four vertical columns and fourteen horizontal, or fifty-six blocks, including everything. The table for the Willis odontograph, as published in his book,* has nine vertical columns and twenty-eight horizontal, or 250 blocks for figures. As printed on the card which accompanies the brass instrument, it has fourteen vertical columns and thirty horizontal ones, or 420 blocks for figures. The tables for the new instrument, that for radial flanks and epicycloidal teeth, has fourteen vertical columns and twenty-six horizontal ones, or 304 blocks for figures; or, adding those for table for internal gearing, we get 353. It is believed also, that table I might be reduced by cutting out about half of the horizontal columns, and still

* Willis, p. 137.

the gaps to be filled, in practice, by interpolation be no greater than in the tables for the Willis instrument. This would reduce the tables for the new odontograph, for epicycloidal and rack and pinion gearing to 182 blocks for figures. Then adding the seventy-three blocks for figures in tables II and III, we have the tables for applying the new instrument to all ordinary forms of gears occupying 255 blocks for figures, a number of places much less than is found in the tables on the printed card accompanying the Willis instrument, and but few more than given in the tables published in Professor Willis' book. Taking the table that accompanies the instrument, as the one which it is fair to compare with, we find the tables for the new instrument most compact.

Comparing the instruments themselves for compactness, we see, by reference to the figures, that the modified Willis instrument is a little ahead, though either this, or the new one, may be carried under the tuck of a common pocket-book. In this regard, either of the new instruments possess a degree of portability and ready usefulness, not common to an instrument 6 × 14 inches, as in the older form of odontograph. In fact the new and modified instruments might be treated as mere "pocket pieces," the accompanying tables being recorded in a note-book. This matter of compactness of tables and instruments is, however, only of secondary importance when *counterposed* with desirable results and facility of obtaining them.

These comparisons indicate that the modified Willis odontograph has advantages in the minor points of compactness of instrument and tables. But in the more essential qualities of simplicity of application, the new instrument, as above pointed out, appears to be superior in the ratio of six to eight or nine ; and of form of tooth, superior in the almost mathematical correctness of the curves for faces, and in having radial flanks, as indicated by Figs. 1, 2, 11, 12, and 13. Designers of gearing, familiar with properly formed gear teeth, however much they may admire the short-cuts secured by odontographs, will undoubtedly deprecate the angularity of junction of flanks and faces found in the Willis tooth, and the rude approximation to correct tooth curves inseparable from the circle arc. The excessively thick base of tooth found in Fig. 1, 11, and 13 are undesirable features.

Fig. 12, as compared with Figs. 11 and 13, shows superiority in form of tooth, which, by those who advocate the common form of radial flanks at least, cannot be questioned. This superiority of form of tooth, added to the compactness of instrument and especially to the important advantage possessed by it of great facility of application, will, it is believed, merit for the new odontograph decided preferences.

Fig. 11.

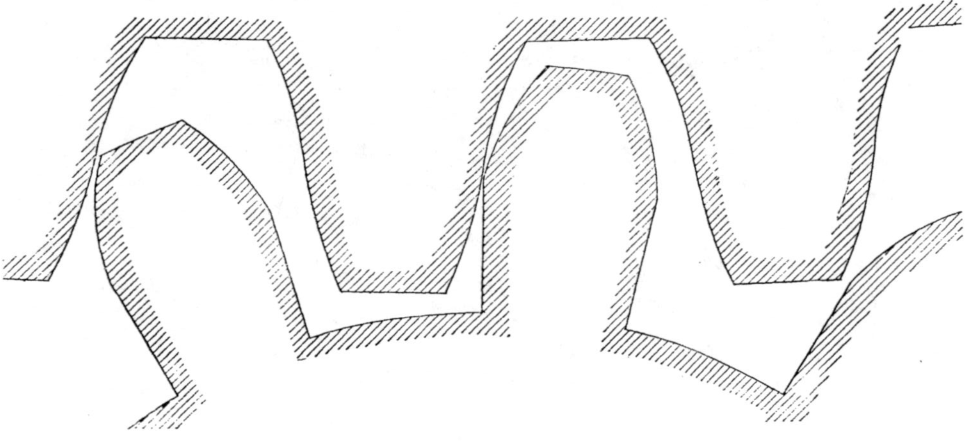

Fig. 12.

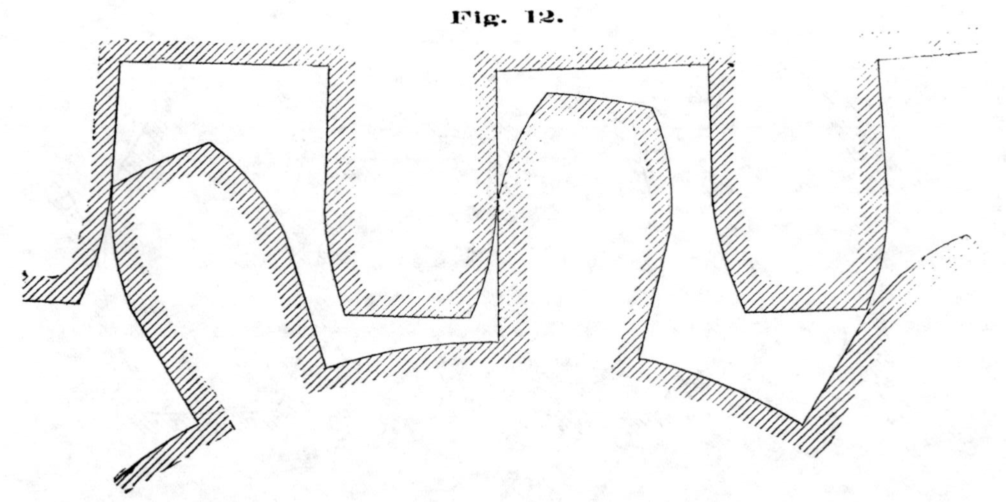

Fig. 13.

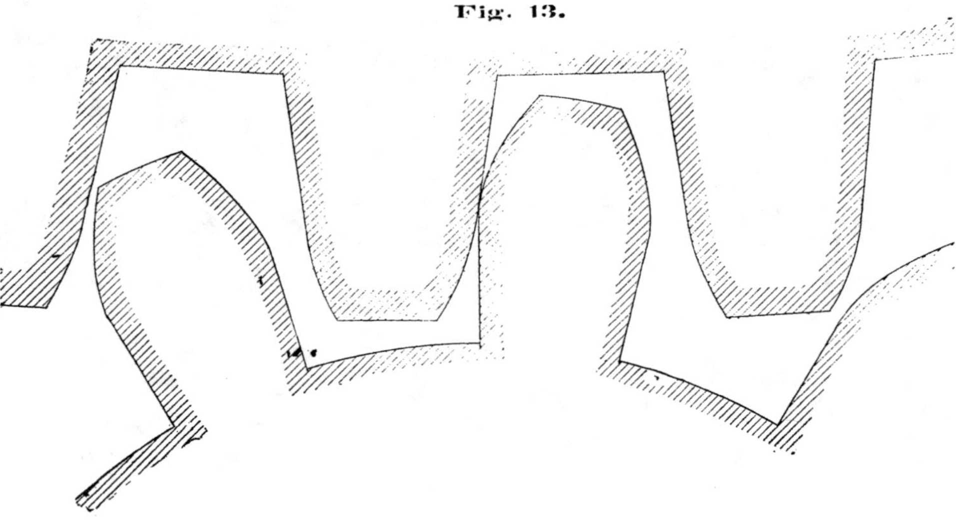

**** Any book in this Catalogue sent free by mail on receipt of price.*

VALUABLE

SCIENTIFIC BOOKS,

PUBLISHED BY

D. VAN NOSTRAND,

23 MURRAY STREET AND 27 WARREN STREET,

NEW YORK.

FRANCIS. Lowell Hydraulic Experiments, being a selection from Experiments on Hydraulic Motors, on the Flow of Water over Weirs, in Open Canals of Uniform Rectangular Section, and through submerged Orifices and diverging Tubes. Made at Lowell, Massachusetts. By James B. Francis, C. E. 2d edition, revised and enlarged, with many new experiments, and illustrated with twenty-three copperplate engravings. 1 vol. 4to, cloth........................$15 00

ROEBLING (J. A.) Long and Short Span Railway Bridges. By John A. Roebling, C. E. Illustrated with large copperplate engravings of plans and views. Imperial folio, cloth.............................. 25 00

CLARKE (T. C.) Description of the Iron Railway Bridge over the Mississippi River, at Quincy, Illinois. Thomas Curtis Clarke, Chief Engineer. Illustrated with 21 lithographed plans. 1 vol. 4to, cloth.. 7 50

TUNNER (P.) A Treatise on Roll-Turning for the Manufacture of Iron. By Peter Tunner. Translated and adapted by John B. Pearse, of the Pennylvania Steel Works, with numerous engravings wood cuts and folio atlas of plates.................$10 0

ISHERWOOD (B. F.) Engineering Precedents for Steam Machinery. Arranged in the most practical and useful manner for Engineers. By B. F. Isherwood, Civil Engineer, U. S. Navy. With Illustrations. Two volumes in one. 8vo, cloth........... $2 50

GILLMORE (Gen. Q. A,) Practical Treatise on the Construction of Roads, Streets, and Pavements. By Q. A. Gillmore, Lt.-Col. U. S Corps of Engineers, Brevet Major-Gen. U. S. Army. With 70 illustrations. 12mo, cloth.................................. 2 00

—— Report on Strength of the Building Stones in the United States, etc. 8vo, illustrated, cloth..... .... 1 50

CAMPIN on the Construction of Iron Roofs. By Francis Campin. 8vo, with plates, cloth........... 2 00

COLLINS. The Private Book of Useful Alloys and Memoranda for Goldsmiths, Jewellers, &c. By James E. Collins. 18mo, cloth.................... 75

CIPHER AND SECRET LETTER AND TELEGRAPHIC CODE, with Hogg's Improvements. The most perfect secret code ever invented or discovered. Impossible to read without the key. By C. S. Larrabee. 18mo, cloth..................... 00

COLBURN. The Gas Works of London. By Zerah Colburn, C. E. 1 vol 12mo, boards.............. 60

CRAIG (B. F.) Weights and Measures. An account of the Decimal System, with Tables of Conversion for Commercial and Scientific Uses. By B. F. Craig, M.D. 1 vol. square 32mo, limp cloth.... 50

NUGENT. Treatise on Optics; or, Light and Sight, theoretically and practically treated; with the application to Fine Art and Industrial Pursuits. By E. Nugent. With one hundred and three illustrations. 12mo, cloth...................................... 1 50

FREE HAND DRAWING. A Guide to Ornamental Figure and Landscape Drawing. By an Art Student. 18mo, boards,.............................. 50

HOWARD. Earthwork Mensuration on the Basis of the Prismoidal Formulae. Containing simple and labor-saving method of obtaining Prismoidal contents directly from End Areas. Illustrated by Examples, and accompanied by Plain Rules for Practical Uses. By Conway R. Howard, C. E., Richmond, Va. Illustrated, 8vo, cloth.............................. 1 50

GRUNER. The Manufacture of Steel. By M. L. Gruner. Translated from the French, by Lenox Smith, with an appendix on the Bessamer process in the United States, by the translator. Illustrated by Lithographed drawings and wood cuts. 8vo, cloth.. 3 50

AUCHINCLOSS. Link and Valve Motions Simplified. Illustrated with 37 wood-cuts, and 21 lithographic plates, together with a Travel Scale, and numerous useful Tables. By W. S. Auchincloss. 8vo, cloth.. 3 00

VAN BUREN. Investigations of Formulas, for the strength of the Iron parts of Steam Machinery. By J. D. Van Buren, Jr., C. E. Illustrated, 8vo, cloth. 2 00

JOYNSON. Designing and Construction of Machine Gearing. Illustrated, 8vo, cloth.................. 2 00

GILLMORE. Coignet Beton and other Artificial Stone. By Q. A. Gillmore, Major U. S. Corps Engineers. 9 plates, views, &c. 8vo, cloth.................... 2 50

SAELTZER. Treattse on Acoustics in connection with Ventilation. By Alexander Saeltzer, Architect. 12mo, cloth.................................. 2 00

BUTLER (W. F.) Ventilation of Buildings. By W. F. Butler. With illustrations. 18mo, boards......... 50

DICTIONARY of Manufactures, Mining, Machinery, and the Industrial Arts. By George Dodd. 12mo, cloth.. 1 50

BOW. A Treatise on Bracing, with its application to Bridges and other Structures of Wood or Iron. By Robert Henry Bow, C. E. 156 illustrations, 8vo, cloth.. 1 50

BARBA (J.) The Use of Steel for Constructive Purposes; Method of Working, Applying, and Testing Plates and Brass. With a Preface by A. L. Holley, C. E. 12mo, cloth............................... 1 50

GILLMORE (Gen. Q. A.) Treatise on Limes, Hydraulic Cements, and Mortars. Papers on Practical Engineering, U. S. Engineer Department, No. 9, containing Reports of numerous Experiments conducted in New York City, during the years 1858 to 1861, inclusive. By Q. A. Gillmore, Bvt. Maj.-Gen., U. S. A., Major, Corps of Engineers. With numerous illustrations. 1 vol, 8vo, cloth.............. $4 00

HARRISON. The Mechanic's Tool Book, with Practical Rules and Suggestions for Use of Machinists, Iron Workers, and others. By W. B. Harrison, associate editor of the "American Artisan." Illustrated with 44 engravings. 12mo, cloth............ 1 50

HENRICI (Olaus). Skeleton Structures, especially in their application to the Building of Steel and Iron Bridges. By Olaus Henrici. With folding plates and diagrams. 1 vol. 8vo, cloth.................... 1 50

HEWSON (Wm.) Principles and Practice of Embanking Lands from River Floods, as applied to the Levees of the Mississippi. By William Hewson, Civil Engineer. 1 vol. 8vo, cloth...................... 2 00

HOLLEY (A. L.) Railway Practice. American and European Railway Practice, in the economical Generation of Steam, including the Materials and Construction of Coal-burning Boilers, Combustion, the Variable Blast, Vaporization, Circulation, Superheating, Supplying and Heating Feed-water, etc., and the Adaptation of Wood and Coke-burning Engines to Coal-burning; and in Permanent Way, including Road-bed, Sleepers, Rails, Joint-fastenings, Street Railways, etc., etc. By Alexander L. Holley, B. P. With 77 lithographed plates. 1 vol. folio, cloth.... 12 00

KING (W. H.) Lessons and Practical Notes on Steam, the Steam Engine, Propellers, etc., etc., for Young Marine Engineers, Students, and others. By the late W. H. King, U. S. Navy. Revised by Chief Engineer J. W. King, U. S. Navy. Nineteenth edition, enlarged. 8vo, cloth...................... 2 00

MINIFIE (Wm.) Mechanical Drawing. A Text-Book of Geometrical Drawing for the use of Mechanics and Schools, in which the Definitions and Rules of Geometry are familiarly explained; the Practical Problems are arranged, from the most simple to the more complex, and in their description technicalities are avoided as much as possible. With illustrations for Drawing Plans, Sections, and Elevations of Buildings and Machinery; an Introduction to Isometrical Drawing, and an Essay on Linear Perspective and Shadows. Illustrated with over 200 diagrams engraved on steel. By Wm. Minifie, Architect. Ninth edition. With an Appendix on the Theory and Application of Colors. 1 vol. 8vo, cloth.............. $4 00

"It is the best work on Drawing that we have ever seen, and is especially a text-book of Geometrical Drawing for the use of Mechanics and Schools. No young Mechanic, such as a Machinists, Engineer, Cabinet-maker, Millwright, or Carpenter, should be without it."—*Scientific American.*

—— Geometrical Drawing. Abridged from the octavo edition, for the use of Schools. Illustrated with 48 steel plates. Fifth edition. 1 vol. 12mo, cloth.... 2 00

STILLMAN (Paul.) Steam Engine Indicator, and the Improved Manometer Steam and Vacuum Gauges—their Utility and Application. By Paul Stillman. New edition. 1 vol. 12mo, flexible cloth........... 1 00

SWEET (S. H.) Special Report on Coal; showing its Distribution, Classification, and cost delivered over different routes to various points in the State of New York, and the principal cities on the Atlantic Coast. By S. H. Sweet. With maps, 1 vol. 8vo, cloth..... 3 00

WALKER (W. H.) Screw Propulsion. Notes on Screw Propulsion: its Rise and History. By Capt. W. H. Walker, U. S. Navy. 1 vol. 8vo, cloth..... 75

WARD (J. H.) Steam for the Million. A popular Treatise on Steam and its Application to the Useful Arts, especially to Navigation. By J. H. Ward, Commander U. S. Navy. New and revised edition. 1 vol. 8vo, cloth.................................. 1 00

WIESBACH (Julius). A Manual of Theoretical Mechanics. By Julius Weisbach, Ph. D. Translated from the fourth augmented and improved German edition, with an Introduction to the Calculus, by Eckley B. Coxe, A. M., Mining Engineer. 1,100 pages, and 902 wood-cut illustrations. 8vo, cloth......... 10 00

DIEDRICH. The Theory of Strains, a Compendium for the calculation and construction of Bridges, Roofs, and Cranes, with the application of Trigonometrical Notes, containing the most comprehensive information in regard to the Resulting strains for a permanent Load, as also for a combined (Permanent and Rolling) Load. In two sections, adadted to the requirements of the present time. By John Diedrich, C. E. Illustrated by numerous plates and diagrams. 8vo, cloth.................................... 5 00

WILLIAMSON (R. S.) On the use of the Barometer on Surveys and Reconnoissances. Part I. Meteorology in its Connection with Hypsometry. Part II. Barometric Hypsometry. By R. S. Wiliamson, Bvt Lieut.-Col. U. S. A., Major Corps of Engineers. With Illustrative Tables and Engravings. Paper No. 15, Professional Papers, Corps of Engineers. 1 vol. 4to, cloth.................................. 15 00

POOK (S. M.) Method of Comparing the Lines and Draughting Vessels Propelled by Sail or Steam. Including a chapter on Laying off on the Mould-Loft Floor. By Samuel M. Pook, Naval Constructor. 1 vol. 8vo, with illustrations, cloth............ 5 00

ALEXANDER (J. H.) Universal Dictionary of Weights and Measures, Ancient and Modern, reduced to the standards of the United States of America. By J. H. Alexander. New edition, enlarged. 1 vol. 8vo, cloth.................................. 3 50

WANKLYN. A Practical Treatise on the Examination of Milk, and its Derivatives, Cream, Butter and Cheese. By J. Alfred Wanklyn, M. R. C. S., 12mo, cloth.. 1 00

RICHARDS' INDICATOR. A Treatise on the Richards Steam Engine Indicator, with an Appendix by F. W. Bacon, M. E. 18mo, flexible, cloth.......... 1 00

PORTER (C. T.) A Treatise on the Richards Steam Engine Indicator, and the Development and Application of Force in the Steam Engine. By Charles T. Porter. Third edition, revised and enlarged. 8vo, illustrated, cloth.................................. 3 50

POPE. Modern Practice of the Electric Telegraph. A Hand Book for Electricians and operators. By Frank L. Pope. Ninth edition, revised and enlarged, and fully illustrated. 8vo, cloth $2 00

"There is no other work of this kind in the English language that contains in so small a compass so much practical information in the application of galvanic electricity to telegraphy. It should be in the hands of every one interested in telegraphy, or the use of Batteries for other purposes."

EASSIE (P. B.) Wood and its Uses. A Hand-Book for the use of Contractors, Builders, Architects, Engineers, and Timber Merchants. By P. B. Eassie. Upwards of 250 illustrations. 8vo, cloth 1 50

SABINE. History and Progress of the Electric Telegraph, with descriptions of some of the apparatus. By Robert Sabine, C. E. Second edition, with additions, 12mo, cloth 1 25

BLAKE. Ceramic Art. A Report on Pottery, Porcelain, Tiles, Terra Cotta and Brick. By W. P. Blake, U. S. Commissioner, Vienna Exhibition, 1873. 8vo, cloth 2 00

BENET. Electro-Ballistic Machines, and the Schultz Chronoscope. By Lieut.-Col. S. V. Benet, Captain of Ordnance, U. S. Army. Illustrated, second edition, 4to, cloth 3 00

MICHAELIS. The Le Boulenge Chronograph, with three Lithograph folding plates of illustrations. By Brevet Captain O. E. Michaelis, First Lieutenant Ordnance Corps, U. S. Army, 4to, cloth 3 00

ENGINEERING FACTS AND FIGURES An Annual Register of Progress in Mechanical Engineering and Construction. for the years 1863, 64, 65, 66, 67, 68. Fully illustrated, 6 vols. 18mo, cloth, $2.50 per vol., each volume sold separately..............

HAMILTON. Useful Information for Railway Men. Compiled by W. G. Hamilton, Engineer. Sixth edition, revised and enlarged, 562 pages Pocket form. Morocco, gilt 2 00

STUART (B.) How to Become a Successful Engineer. Being Hints to Youths intending to adopt the Profession. Sixth edition. 12mo, boards 50

STUART. The Civil and Military Engineers of America. By Gen. C. B. Stuart. With 9 finely executed portraits of eminent engineers, and illustrated by engravings of some of the most important works constructed in America. 8vo, cloth.................. $5 00

STONEY. The Theory of Strains in Girders and similar structures, with observations on the application of Theory to Practice, and Tables of Strength and other properties of Materials. By Bindon B. Stoney, B. A. New and revised edition, enlarged, with numerous engravings on wood, by Oldham. Royal 8vo, 664 pages. Complete in one volume. 8vo, cloth....... 12 50

SHREVE. A Treatise on the Strength of Bridges and Roofs. Comprising the determination of Algebraic formulas for strains in Horizontal, Inclined or Rafter, Triangular, Bowstring, Lenticular and other Trusses, from fixed and moving loads, with practical applications and examples, for the use of Students and Engineers. By Samuel H. Shreve, A. M., Civil Engineer. 87 wood-cut illustrations. 2d edition. 8vo, cloth... 5 00

MERRILL. Iron Truss Bridges for Railroads. The method of calculating strains in Trusses, with a careful comparison of the most prominent Trusses, in reference to economy in combination, etc., etc. By Brevet Col. William E. Merrill, U S. A., Major Corps of Engineers, with nine lithographed plates of Illustrations. 4to, cloth.......................... 5 00

WHIPPLE. An Elementary and Practical Treatise on Bridge Building. An enlarged and improved edition of the author's original work. By S. Whipple, C. E., inventor of the Whipple Bridges, &c. Illustrated 8vo, cloth.. 4 00

THE KANSAS CITY BRIDGE. With an account of the Regimen of the Missouri River, and a description of the methods used for Founding in that River. By O. Chanute, Chief Engineer, and George Morrison, Assistant Engineer. Illustrated with five lithographic views and twelve plates of plans. 4to, cloth, 6 00

DUBOIS (A. J.) The New Method of Graphical Statics. By A. J. Dubois, C. E., Ph. D. With 60 illustrations. 8vo, cloth 2 00

MAC CORD. A Practical Treatise on the Slide Valve by Eccentrics, examining by methods the action of the Eccentric upon the Slide Valve, and explaining the Practical processes of laying out the movements, adapting the valve for its various duties in the steam engine. For the use of Engineers, Draughtsmen, Machinists, and Students of Valve Motions in general. By C. W. Mac Cord, A. M., Professor of Mechanical Drawing, Stevens' Institute of Technology, Hoboken, N. J. Illustrated by 8 full page copper-plates. 4to, cloth.................................. $3 00

KIRKWOOD. Report on the Filtration of River Waters, for the supply of cities, as practised in Europe, made to the Board of Water Commissioners of the City of St. Louis. By James P. Kirkwood. Illustrated by 30 double plate engravings. 4to, cloth, 15 00

PLATTNER. Manual of Qualitative and Quantitative Analysis with the Blow Pipe. From the last German edition, revised and enlarged. By Prof. Th. Richter. of the Royal Saxon Mining Academy. Translated by Prof. H. B. Cornwall, Assistant in the Columbia School of Mines, New York assisted by John H. Caswell. Illustrated with 87 wood cuts, and one lithographic plate. Third edition, revised, 560 pages, 8vo, cloth.. 7 50

PLYMPTON. The Blow Pipe. A Guide to its Use in the Determination of Salts and Minerals. Compiled from various sources, by George W. Plympton, C. E. A. M., Professor of Physical Science in the Polytechnic Institute, Brooklyn, New York, 12mo, cloth.. 1 50

PYNCHON. Introduction to Chemical Physics, designed for the use of Academies, Colleges and High Schools. Illustrated with numerous engravings, and containing copious experiments with directions for preparing them. By Thomas Ruggles Pynchon, M. A., Professor of Chemistry and the Natural Sciences, Trinity College, Hartford New edition, revised and enlarged and illustrated by 269 illustrations on wood. Crown, 8vo. cloth........................ 3 00

ELIOT AND STORER. A compendious Manual of Qualitative Chemical Analysis. By Charles W. Eliot and Frank H. Storer. Revised with the Co-operation of the authors. By William R. Nichols, Professor of Chemistry in the Massachusetts Institute of Technology Illustrated, 12mo, cloth....... $1 50

RAMMELSBERG. Guide to a course of Quantitative Chemical Analysis. especially of Minerals and Furnace Products. Illustrated by Examples By C. F. Rammelsberg. Translated by J. Towler, M. D. 8vo, cloth.................................... 2 25

DOUGLASS and PRESCOTT. Qualitative Chemical Analysis. A Guide in the Practical Study of Chemistry, and in the Work of Analysis. By S. H. Douglass and A. B Prescott, of the University of Michigan. New edition. 8vo. *In press.*

JACOB. On the Designing and Construction of Storage Reservoirs, with Tables and Wood Cuts representing Sections, &c , 18mo, boards............... 50

WATT'S Dictionary of Chemistry. New and Revised edition complete in 6 vols 8vo cloth, $62.00 Supplementary volume sold separately. Price, cloth... 9 00

RANDALL. Quartz Operators Hand-Book. By P. M. Randall. New edition, revised and enlarged, fully illustrated. 12mo, cloth 2 00

SILVERSMITH. A Practical Hand-Book for Miners, Metallurgists, and Assayers, comprising the most recent improvements in the disintegration amalgamation, smelting, and parting of the Precious ores, with a comprehensive Digest of the Mining Laws. Greatly augmented, revised and corrected. By Julius Silversmith. Fourth edition. Profusely illustrated. 12mo, cloth....................................... 3 00

THE USEFUL METALS AND THEIR ALLOYS, including Mining Ventilation, Mining Jurisprudence, and Metallurgic Chemistry employed in the conversion of Iron, Copper, Tin, Zinc, Antimony and Lead ores, with their applications to the Industrial Arts. By Scoffren, Truan, Clay, Oxland, Fairbairn, and others. Fifth edition, half calf..................... 3 75

JOYNSON. The Metals used in construction, Iron, Steel, Bessemer Metal, etc., etc. By F. H. Joynson. Illustrated, 12mo, cloth.......................... $0 75

VON COTTA. Treatise on Ore Deposits. By Bernhard Von Cotta, Professor of Geology in the Royal School of Mines, Freidberg, Saxony. Translated from the second German edition, by Frederick Prime, Jr., Mining Engineer, and revised by the author, with numerous illustrations. 8vo, cloth....... 4 00

GREENE. Graphical Method for the Analysis of Bridge Trusses, extended to continuous Girders and Draw Spans. By C. E. Greene, A. M., Prof. of Civil Engineering, University of Michigan. Illustrated by 3 folding plates, 8vo, cloth.......................... 2 00

BELL. Chemical Phenomena of Iron Smelting. An experimental and practical examination of the circumstances which determine the capacity of the Blast Furnace, The Temperature of the air, and the proper condition of the Materials to be operated upon. By I. Lowthian Bell. 8vo, cloth........... 6 00

ROGERS. The Geology of Pennsylvania. A Government survey, with a general view of the Geology of the United States, Essays on the Coal Formation and its Fossils, and a description of the Coal Fields of North America and Great Britain. By Henry Darwin Rogers, late State Geologist of Pennsylvania, Splendidly illustrated with Plates and Engravings in the text. 3 vols., 4to, cloth with Portfolio of Maps. 30 00

BURGH. Modern Marine Engineering, applied to Paddle and Screw Propulsion. Consisting of 36 colored plates, 259 Practical Wood Cut Illustrations, and 403 pages of descriptive matter, the whole being an exposition of the present practice of James Watt & Co., J. & G Rennie, R. Napier & Sons, and other celebrated firms, by N. P. Burgh, Engineer, thick 4to, vol., cloth, $25.00; half mor........ 30 00

CHURCH. Notes of a Metallurgical Journey in Europe. By J. A. Church, Engineer of Mines, 8vo, cloth..... 2 00

BOURNE. Treatise on the Steam Engine in its various applications to Mines, Mills, Steam Navigation, Railways, and Agriculture, with the theoretical investigations respecting the Motive Power of Heat, and the proper proportions of steam engines. Elaborate tables of the right dimensions of every part, and Practical Instructions for the manufacture and management of every species of Engine in actual use. By John Bourne, being the ninth edition of "A Treatise on the Steam Engine," by the "Artizan Club." Illustrated by 38 plates and 546 wood cuts. 4to, cloth.. $15 00

STUART. The Naval Dry Docks of the United States. By Charles B. Stuart late Engineer-in-Chief of the U. S. Navy. Illustrated with 24 engravings on steel. Fourth edition, cloth.................... 6 00

ATKINSON. Practical Treatises on the Gases met with in Coal Mines. 18mo, boards................ 50

FOSTER. Submarine Blasting in Boston Harbor, Massachusetts. Removal of Tower and Corwin Rocks. By J. G. Foster, Lieut.-Col. of Engineers, U. S. Army. Illustrated with seven plates, 4to, cloth.. 3 50

BARNES Submarine Warfare, offensive and defensive, including a discussion of the offensive Torpedo System, its effects upon Iron Clad Ship Systems and influence upon future naval wars. By Lieut.-Commander J. S. Barnes, U. S. N., with twenty lithographic plates and many wood cuts. 8vo, cloth..... 5 00

HOLLEY. A Treatise on Ordnance and Armor, embracing descriptions, discussions, and professional opinions concerning the materials, fabrication, requirements, capabilities, and endurance of European and American Guns, for Naval, Sea Coast, and Iron Clad Warfare, and their Rifling, Projectiles, and Breech-Loading; also, results of experiments against armor, from official records, with an appendix referring to Gun Cotton, Hooped Guns, etc., etc. By Alexander L. Holley, B. P., 948 pages, 493 engravings, and 147 Tables of Results, etc., 8vo, half roan. 10 00

SIMMS. A Treatise on the Principles and Practice of Levelling, showing its application to purposes of Railway Engineering and the Construction of Roads, &c. By Frederick W. Simms, C. E. From the 5th London edition, revised and corrected, with the addition of Mr. Laws's Practical Examples for setting out Railway Curves. Illustrated with three Lithographic plates and numerous wood cuts. 8vo, cloth. $2 50

BURT. Key to the Solar Compass, and Surveyor's Companion; comprising all the rules necessary for use in the field; also description of the Linear Surveys and Public Land System of the United States, Notes on the Barometer, suggestions for an outfit for a survey of four months, etc By W. A. Burt, U. S. Deputy Surveyor. Second edition. Pocket book form, tuck.. 2 50

THE PLANE TABLE. Its uses in Topographical Surveying, from the Papers of the U. S. Coast Survey. Illustrated, 8vo, cloth....................... 2 00

"This work gives a description of the Plane Table, employed at the U. S. Coast Survey office, and the manner of using it."

JEFFER'S. Nautical Surveying. By W. N. Jeffers, Captain U. S. Navy. Illustrated with 9 copperplates and 31 wood cut illustrations. 8vo, cloth.......... 5 00

CHAUVENET. New method of correcting Lunar Distances, and improved method of Finding the error and rate of a chronometer, by equal altitudes. By W. Chauvenet, LL.D. 8vo, cloth................. 2 00

BRUNNOW. Spherical Astronomy. By F. Brunnow, Ph. Dr. Translated by the author from the second German edition. 8vo, cloth...................... 6 50

PEIRCE. System of Analytic Mechanics. By Benjamin Peirce. 4to, cloth.......................... 10 00

COFFIN. Navigation and Nautical Astronomy. Prepared for the use of the U. S. Naval Academy. By Prof. J. H. C. Coffin. Fifth edition. 52 wood cut illustrations. 12mo, cloth.......................... 3 50

NOBLE (W. H.) Useful Tables. Compiled by W. H. Noble, M. A., Captain Royal Artillery. Pocket form, cloth.................................... 50

CLARK. Theoretical Navigation and Nautical Astronomy. By Lieut. Lewis Clark, U. S. N. Illustrated with 41 wood cuts. 8vo, cloth $3 00

HASKINS. The Galvanometer and its Uses. A Manual for Electricians and Students. By C. H. Haskins. 12mo, pocket form, morocco. 2 00

MORRIS (E.) Easy Rules for the Measurement of Earthworks, by Means of the Prismoidal Formula. By Ellwood Morris, C. E. 78 illustrations. 8vo, cloth 1 50

BECKWITH. Observations on the Materials and Manufacture of Terra-Cotta, Stone Ware, Fire Brick, Porcelain and Encaustic Tiles, with remarks on the products exhibited at the London International Exhibition, 1871. By Arthur Beckwith, C. E. 8vo, paper 60

MORFIT. A Practical Treatise on Pure Fertilizers, and the chemical conversion of Rock Guano, Marlstones, Coprolites. and the Crude Phosphates of Lime and Alumina generally, into various valuable products. By Campbell Morfit, M.D., with 28 illustrative plates, 8vo, cloth 20 00

BARNARD. The Metric System of Weights and Measures. An address delivered before the convocation of the University of the State of New York, at Albany, August, 1871. By F. A. P. Barnard, LL.D., President of Columbia College, New York. Second edition from the revised edition, printed for the Trustees of Columbia College. Tinted paper, 8vo, cloth 3 00

—— Report on Machinery and Processes on the Industrial Arts and Apparatus of the Exact Sciences. By F. A. P. Barnard, LL.D. Paris Universal Exposition, 1867. Illustrated, 8vo, cloth.............. 5 00

ALLAN. Theory of Arches. By Prof. W. Allan, formerly of Washington & Lee University, 18mo, b'rds 50

ALLAN (Prof W.) Strength of Beams under Transverse Loads. By Prof. W. Allan, author of "Theory of Arches." With illustrations. 18mo, boards..... 50

www.ingramcontent.com/pod-product-compliance
Lightning Source LLC
LaVergne TN
LVHW021408110826
845150LV00007B/1836